BIG FISH
From Famous Waters

BIG FISH
From Famous Waters

Compiled by Chris Turnbull

DAVID & CHARLES
Newton Abbot   London

This book is dedicated to Jade Rose and to all the other children of the eighties, in the hope that they may grow up to inherit clean, clear, glistening waters and that they will be prepared to fight to keep them unspoiled and capable of becoming legends.

British Library Cataloguing in Publication Data

Big fish from famous waters.
1. Great Britain. Freshwater angling
I. Turnbull, Chris
799.110941

ISBN 0-7153-9453-3

Typeset by Typesetters (Birmingham) Ltd, Smethwick, West Midlands and printed in Singapore by C S Graphics Pte Ltd

for David & Charles plc
Brunel House   Newton Abbot   Devon

Contents

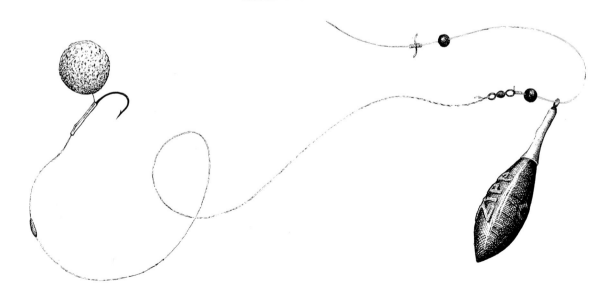

Chris Turnbull 89.

Introduction

Chris Turnbull

Looking back over thirty years to my childhood efforts at catching tench from my local millpond, I remember our first all-night vigils spent striking line-bites, not only from fish hitting the line but also from bats hunting the swarms of nocturnal insects drawn to the blacked-out hurricane lamps which we used to illuminate our swingtips. I also remember the night when my companion, Dick Hewit, had his rod almost dragged from the rests by our first carp. It was a beautiful creature weighing all of 3lb 14oz, a common, with huge glistening scales the size of sixpenny bits. That night we laughed and joked each time another 2lb tench joined the carp in the nets: 'Watch out Walker, roll over Taylor', we jested in jubilation at our success and in innocent mockery of our heroes.

It would have been during the long school holidays of 1963. We had been reared on Bernard Venables' book, *Mr Crabtree Goes Fishing*. The fictitious Crabtree, however, had now been knocked from his pedestal by new angling heroes. Richard Walker, Fred Taylor and Peter Stone were the names which had upstaged our old master and it was their exploits which we now sought to emulate and perhaps even outshine.

Of course, that old millpond in Sussex would never be able to provide us with the opportunities which Walker had encountered at Redmire but we could play and pretend, we could even believe that there was a record carp or two swimming there. Even if such a fish had existed, there was no way we could ever have landed it but we were now firmly caught by the wave of grandeur as this new, big-fish scene flushed over the angling world. In our imagination, at least, we were going to match our new heroes.

I don't know what happened to my old companions or if any of them still fish for those big fish of our dreams. As for myself, I slowly realised, as I grew older, that if I really wanted to come to terms with some of these lunkers, I would have to move onto waters more capable of growing them. Nearly two decades later that realisation had me fishing some of the best big-fish waters in the country. Through the eighties I spent many hours, days, weeks and more, casting my lines on these waters which had gained very special reputations. Waters such as the River Wensum and the Avon, the Broads of the Upper Thurne, Redmire Pool, the reservoirs at Ardleigh and Llandegfedd, Johnsons Lakes and others. Friendships were made with many brilliant anglers around the country and it was on these waters and from these friendships that the concept of this book grew.

This book is an attempt to chronicle the highest moments and achievements of Britain's specimen-hunting movement throughout the eighties, a decade which in angling history surely is unparalleled by any before. Few books have been written which focus on a particular fishery, or on the stories of the highly successful anglers who fished there, or the fabulous fish that were caught. What massive potential such a theme holds. The prime objective of *Big Fish* is to expand on this theme by taking an

Chris Turnbull 89

in-depth look at a handful of extraordinary fisheries which, throughout the eighties, constantly stole the headlines of the angling press. In doing so it tells many of the greatest angling success stories of the decade.

No modern angler with an interest in big fish could have failed to be aware of these waters or of the massive fish with which they have become synonymous. Not surprisingly these fisheries stole the imagination of the angling world in general and also drew the attention of some of our finest specimen-hunters, men who are ever alert to the opportunity of tackling the ultimate possibilities their sport has to offer. With the best of the country's anglers on the best of its waters, one thing you can depend on is that history will be in the making.

These anglers, the cream of the specimen scene, are constantly in the public eye. For some of them, their involvement in big-fish angling is so serious that it has become an integral part of their life-style. At its most intense this search for the ultimate specimen can become a total obsession, a quest for the piscatorial Holy Grail. Extreme though such an approach may be, if they are to be truly successful rather than occasionally lucky, this may be the level of dedication these waters can dictate, for really big fish are few and far between and success, if it is to come, will be hard won and seldom repeated. Once achieved, however, success will be the ultimate reward, maybe the fruit of many weeks, months or even years of effort. It may be enough to build a man's reputation to legendary status, it may even be enough to turn a new page in angling history, for such waters can produce records, thus setting a new pinnacle in angling achievement. Few may do so time after time. These fisheries are not ordinary places, they are the key waters and on their banks the ambitions of a generation of big-fish specialists have been sought and occasionally have been attained.

There have, of course, always been key waters which earn a special place in angling history, but it is perhaps only since the early fifties, at the dawn of the big-fish scene, that their significance and potential were brought fully into context. This recognition was explicitly pushed upon the angling world by the fantastic exploits of that great patron of the movement, the late Richard Walker. He, above all, proved that big fish could be caught regularly and by design rather than by relying on the whims of luck. In his angling newspaper columns of the fifties he predicted the capture of a new record carp, one so enormous that the angling world of the day just could not accept it. The rest of that story is now history, as in September 1952 Richard made his way to Redmire Pool and from its beautiful depths landed a carp so big that it nearly doubled the weight of the previous record for the species.

Both Walker and Redmire have earned their place as legendary giants in the angling archives. For Walker, perhaps it was his finest hour but for Redmire the story had only just begun. She, of course, went on to become renowned as the most prolific big-carp water in the country and then, almost thirty years after Walker's triumph, went on to provide Chris Yates with a new record of over 50lb in weight.

This, then, is the stuff of which legends are made and upon which the foundations of this book are laid. Flash in the pan leviathans are occasionally caught from all sorts of waters which have no real form and there are undoubtedly many good waters which produce some excellent specimens, but this book is focussed on the excellence of the few superb waters which have proved time after time to offer the very pinnacle of angling potential, the jewels in its crown.

Some of these waters have taken a place at the very heart of angling tradition. The Hampshire Avon and the Broads of Norfolk's Upper Thurne spring readily to mind. They have been legends for as long as anyone can recall. Other waters, in the midst of the eighties, sprang out of the blue and produced some massive fish which shocked the angling world to its roots. Who, for example, could have failed to be stunned by the marvellous achievements of those anglers who, against staggering odds, set out to conquer the record-shattering bream of Oxfordshire's Queenford Lagoon? The headline stories which these waters have spawned through the eighties are not only compelling reading they are legends in their own right.

As it is outside the realms of possibility that any one angler could write knowledgeably or intimately of all these waters, I have gathered together, as contributors, a team of anglers who actually helped to achieve the tremendous potential that each fishery had to offer. These are the very anglers whose depth of experience and knowledge sets them aside as expert authorities on these waters. They are the actual men whose achievements helped ensure these waters' rightful place in this hall of fame.

Big Fish is not another dry, instructive book on fishing, although, in the unfolding, its chapters inevitably touch on the methods, ideas and principles which were used successfully on each water. Neither is it intended to be deeply scientific by delving into a complex analysis of these waters' biology, or the reasons why they have developed into such fabulous places. Far more exciting than any of these things *Big Fish* is, as its title suggests, a collection of great angling adventures. These are the stories of many of the finest achievements of the specimen-hunting fraternity throughout the last decade: a period when this movement came of age, went out and caught far more huge fish and shattered more records than in any previous decade in angling history.

These then are the stories of great anglers, fantastic fish and fabulous waters. Hopefully it is a tribute to them all . . .

Richard Walker with his 1952 record carp

1
Redmire: The Pool of Dreams

Christopher Yates

Redmire, the ultimate angling legend. No other water has stood so large in angling history. Despite its insignificant size, acre for acre this tiny estate lake on the Welsh borderlands has, over the years, produced some mammoth carp and ignited more passions than any other British water. At the top of this incredible list are two records including a 51½-pounder caught in June 1980 by Chris Yates.

Chris is acknowledged as one of the most naturally gifted and successful carp anglers of all and is the only man ever to have landed two different 40lb plus carp from Redmire. More recently he has very successfully turned his attention to fishing for the barbel of the Hampshire Avon.

Chris also must surely rate as one of our finest angling authors. His many writings include his book Casting at the Sun, *a true classic, which in the opinion of many rates as the finest angling book ever published. We can all look forward to his next book due out this year. As one of angling's few true romantics his great affinity with, reverence and knowledge of Redmire, surely makes him the perfect writer for this chapter.*

This was going to be a reasonably conventional, straightforward description of one of the most famous waters of recent angling history. However, I have just got back from a wonderful two weeks at that place – my first visit there for years – and I now find that it's impossible for me to be conventional and straightforward about somewhere that is obviously so magical and extraordinary. It wasn't that I had previously forgotten about these special qualities, it was simply that during my eight-year absence from Redmire I had sobered up: my intoxication by Redmire had worn off.

Just a month ago I could have written a clear-headed, objective chapter, making a pen-portrait of the water and giving a chronological account of the events that had made Redmire famous, flavouring the whole with a few personal experiences. I am once more drunk with Redmire, having had way over the limit of its potent atmosphere. I am, therefore, incapable of driving this vintage fountain pen in a straight line. I promise that I shall, during a quieter moment in this text, touch on a bit of Redmire's history, geography, ecology and even chemistry, but first I have to write about its essential character, its compelling personality, and the qualities that make it entirely different from any other stillwater in the country.

The first thing that strikes you about Redmire when you stand on the dam and look along its length is that it appears too small. Surely a lake with such a reputation should be at least 10 acres, yet it is barely 3 acres. Surely such a diminutive pond could not possibly have produced so many gigantic carp, yet since its 'discovery' in 1951 it has produced scores of 20-pounders, dozens of 'thirties', three 'forties' and a 'fifty'. Add to this the well-documented sighting of several monsters up to possibly 70 or even 80lb and you begin to believe that there must be some powerful magic going on there.

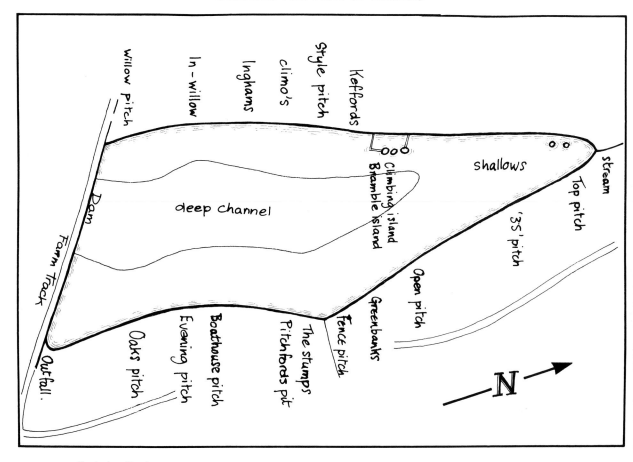

Redmire Pool

The next thing you notice is its perfect setting in the landscape. It lies in a fold of the high, rolling Herefordshire border country, surrounded by trees and thick hedgerows, out of sight of any road or vantage point. When the wind is in the east you can hear the traffic on the Monmouth road but it doesn't really disturb the settled tranquility of the place. Redmire seems a thousand miles from 'civilisation'. It feels even more remote if, at sunset, after the harvest, you climb the gate at the end of the dam and walk up the slope to the top of the barley field. Looking west you will see nothing but lines of hills stretching away from you and in the far distance the long ridge of the Black Mountains.

Redmire's banks are well grown with trees, mostly alder and willow. There are two large, ancient oaks that hang over deep water on the east bank. Beneath these venerable trees the famous nature writer and carp angler, 'B.B.' said he always sensed '. . . a strange stirring in the air'. Many lesser men, including myself, have at certain times noticed a mysterious change in the atmosphere at that same place. I think one of the oaks is haunted. There are also the twin balsam poplars halfway along the east bank whose leaves exhale a lovely, fragrant perfume especially noticeable on calm mornings in early summer. And there are several ash trees, my favourite being the craggy, lichened old specimen that I slept under for several nights last week. It also stands on the east bank, a few yards from the first of the ancient crack willows. (Eighteen years ago, there were many tall, stately elms and also a huge, beautiful weeping willow. The elms fell victim to that devastating plague which altered the appearance of so much of England and the willow died of old age.)

You are getting the feel of Redmire now, becoming accustomed to its physical characteristics and deceptive appearance. But there is something else, an undercurrent of energy or pressure that is Redmire's distinctive atmosphere, an atmosphere that thickens and thins and can charge the most ordinary day with a wonderful sense of expectancy, like the approach of a thunderstorm. Of course, some anglers are not at all interested in such unquantifiable stuff. They are only concerned with accumulating lists of weighty carp and would probably even deny the existence of atmosphere. Yet atmosphere is like mood; you read a person's mood by the expression on his face. You can read Redmire's mood by keeping your mind open and your senses alert and noticing any changes, not in the conditions, but in the atmosphere.

Bob James returns a 20lb Redmire common caught during the filming session in June 1989

Wonderful conditions, wonderful atmosphere, wonderful fishing

Since 1972, when I first fished there, I have spent the equivalent of an entire year at Redmire. In all that time, it was the atmosphere that attracted me most. Eventually, as you know, the best time to ask a favour of a friend is to recognise when he or she is in a good mood. Similarly I know when it is a good time for asking a favour of Redmire, by recognising – by a change in the atmosphere – when she is in a good mood.

Of course you don't have to know or believe in those things. Logic, determination and good fishing will probably catch you more carp in the end. And it's true that every carp lake I know has its own characteristic atmosphere. It's just that Redmire has an atmosphere that is, at times, almost tangible, almost like a human presence. When she is in a good mood wonderful things can happen as long as you are respectful and appreciative. But if she is in a bad mood . . .

I was describing these things to the two friends I was fishing with last week. They didn't exactly scoff, though they chuckled a bit. But then certain uncanny incidents began to happen and now my friends are as convinced as me that Redmire has a very powerful changeable personality. More of this later but now some good, solid reassuring facts of history.

Although Redmire is an artificial pool, formed by damming a stream in a narrow valley, it is very old. There were probably three different stages of construction on the dam, with a hundred years or more between stages. For most of this time the pool was

Yates' record

14

used as a reservoir, supplying pure drinking water to Bernithan Court, a building of medieval origins which stands about a quarter of a mile away, on the valley's eastern slope.

As far as I know, there was no introduction of fish until this century, though eels must always have been present. They run up the River Garron from the Wye and, finding the pool's outlet stream to their liking, they follow its course and eventually slither up the overspill and enter Redmire's crystalline depths. The large population would have provided a convenient food source for the court and as eels make as good a dish as any pike, trout or perch there would have been no need to have stocked the pool artificially. Earlier this century, trout were introduced, but, by all accounts, they didn't prosper very well. The locals, who already enjoyed a bit of unofficial night fishing for the eels, certainly helped in the decline of trout. I think the shoals of gudgeon that now live in Redmire are descendants of the surplus live-baits that the locals used to catch the trout and eels.

There were no carp in the pool until 1934 when the late Donald Leney – the Godfather of carp fishing – introduced fifty small fish, yearlings of the Galician strain which he had personally hand-picked from rearing ponds at a fish farm in Holland. At that time, Leney probably knew more about carp than any other man in the country. Trout rearing was his chief profession but carp were his main interest and his experience with the various strains had shown that the Galician was not only a very beautiful fish when well grown, it was also hardier and longer-lived than other forms of king carp.

The owners of Bernithan had asked for the carp because extensive weed growth was clogging the outlet pipes and so disrupting water supply to the court. It was hoped that the omniverous fish would eat some of the weed but, though they munched a few strands, more effective filters to the pumping gear eventually solved the problem. In the meantime the carp prospered not so much because of the weed but because of the purity and quantity of the water and the rich abundance of invertebrate life (carp fodder) it supported. The fish were left undisturbed for almost twenty years and during that period certain specimens grew at the prodigious rate of between 2 and 4lb a year. By the time the first angler cast a line for them in 1950, several of these carp had reached record proportions.

The first angler to deliberately and officially fish for Redmire carp – he was preceded by local poachers – was not Bob Richards, as popular history states, but a man called Johnson. He was a friend of the owners of the estate and obviously a keen fisherman, for he travelled all the way from his Irish home for two or three attempts at the giants. I have only just been made aware of this fact but, unfortunately, no one knows what adventures befell our pioneering Irishman. Was he successful? Was he pulled in? Did he return to his loughs convinced that the monsters could never be outwitted? Are you still with us, Mr Johnson? If you are, please tell us your tale, for your name has just gone down in history.

A name familiar to all angling archivists and historians is the aforementioned Bob Richards, a Gloucester tobacconist who first fished Redmire in October 1951 and landed a new carp record of 31¼lb, a beautiful fish which beat the previous record, set twenty years earlier, by 5lb.

Events took a rapid turn once the angling world had received this staggering news. Bernard Venables ran a story of the capture for the *Daily Express* and he contacted 'B.B.' with a fuller account. After initial disbelief and a conversation with the captor

Watch out for the scarecrow!

himself, 'B.B.' realised the potential of this unknown pond. He was a member of the Carp Catchers Club, along with the late Richard Walker and half a dozen other well-known names, and by the next season the CCC had gained exclusive rights to fish Redmire. (It was christened 'Redmire' as a blind to the rest of the angling world. 'B.B.' tells me that the name was dreamt up by Walker, but Walker told me that it was 'B.B.'s' idea.)

By the end of that famous summer of 1952, several monster carp had been hooked and lost and a few fish were landed, the biggest being another new record, a colossal common carp of 44lb, caught by Richard Walker. Having always been regarded as one of the most obscure, eccentric and arcane branches of angling, carp fishing was suddenly transformed into something respectable and worthwhile. Thousands of fishermen decided that they wanted a Redmire of their own and dozens of lakes and ponds up and down the country were stocked with carp. However, despite numerous minor and major successes, no one has yet managed to create a carp water to match Redmire. There is probably no other carp water in the world that has produced, naturally, such an astonishing head of big carp per acre of water.

Probably angling's greatest prize: Chris Yates and his 51½lb record carp

The twin balsam poplars

Everyone who fished Redmire during the fifties and early sixties expected the carp record to be broken again. Several monsters had been sighted, carp that might have weighed anything between 40 and 60lb. Walker himself netted a 59lb mirror that had been stranded in the shallows while spawning and he, 'B.B' and others spotted a stupendous fish whose weight just didn't bear thinking about. I, too, have seen such an apparition. In July 1979 an extraordinarily huge carp cruised past me, only 20ft away in fairly shallow, crystal-clear water. The light was good and I saw the monster in vivid detail. Without doubt, that was one of the greatest moments of my life, like seeing the Loch Ness Monster or a flying saucer or the real Father Christmas. Since I began fishing Redmire, in 1972, I had spent more time than almost any other single angler observing the carp, yet I'd never before seen – and never would see again – anything remotely like that incredible creature. How big? You would think me utterly mad if I told you what I thought.

A year after seeing Leviathan (or so I called him) I broke Walker's record with a 51½lb mirror carp. (Much to his delight and satisfaction, I caught the fish on a rod Walker had built himself in 1954!) It looked small by comparison!

Does the monster still exist? Can Redmire produce a fourth record? Stranger things have happened, certainly there are carp swimming there that are over fifty years old. My angling pal Bob James caught one of those ancients last week, a leather of 24lb that, through identification of certain distinguishing features, is known to be the same 20lb leather carp that Maurice Ingham caught in 1954. It is probably one of the original stock fish. So if that old grandfather is still going, why shouldn't the monster also be alive, lying hidden somewhere in one of Redmire's deep gulleys?

As to my trip last week, the first week of the 1989 season, I can only repeat that it was wonderful. I went with Bob James and Hugh Miles, who is one of the best wildlife film-makers in the business with a string of international awards and successes to his name. Hugh wanted to make a film about Redmire and hoped we might provide him with some big carp for his camera. Knowing Redmire's enigmatic nature, I said we shouldn't expect too much, but, as it turned out, she was in a good mood and Hugh got some marvellous footage of *four* 20-pounders. Bob and I had a brace apiece and I also had a brace of double-figure commons. We didn't see any monsters but the trip was a memorable experience. Hugh, who has filmed in some of the most spectacular scenery in the world, from the Andes to the Arctic, was completely enchanted by the place. So impressed was he, that he said it was the best trip he'd ever been on. A handsome compliment to Redmire. I won't reveal anything else which might spoil your enjoyment when the film is finally shown on television – though that won't be until 1991. Just watch out for the scarecrow!

I promised to touch on Redmire's ecology and chemistry. So briefly: as far as the carp are concerned, the most delectable links in the food chain consist of bloodworms and daphnia. Gudgeon are also part of their diet. The bulk of the weed is oxygen-producing, life-supporting hornwort and starwort. Reed mace has recently been introduced and may prove to be a problem, also yellow iris, which should not cause any problems. There is also a filamentous blanket weed, whose name I don't know. The carp seem to eat it as if it were some kind of green blancmange. Carp, gudgeon and eels make up the sole fish population. I spoke of the monster, but the strangest thing I ever saw at Redmire was a terrapin. How did *that* get there?

Chemistry: Redmire is full to the brim with pure, unadulterated H_2O!

2
Kent's Secret Perch Lake
Pete Garvan

One of angling's most well-kept secrets, Furnace Pond, lies deep in the Kentish countryside. During the early eighties it produced an incredible number of truly huge perch to the lucky few who were privileged to fish for them.

One of the first anglers to discover and pioneer the tremendous potential of this fishing was Pete Garvan. Bored with match fishing, he was looking for a new direction for his fishing when he discovered the presence of the perch, thus setting out on one of specialist angling's great adventures. Not only did he bank a staggering succession of enormous specimens but he was also fortunate enough to witness a new British record before eventually the lake went into decline.

Pete is now regarded as a highly successful all-round, big-fish angler who tends to seek out new challenges and avoids the hard-fished waters. Besides his enviable record of big perch, his successes include the capture of numerous big pike and carp, both running to over 30lb and big tench to over 9lb.

Any bait placed close to those branches was certain to be taken

Well hidden and situated deep in the heart of the lovely Kent countryside, close to the sleepy village of Horsmonden, lies Furnace Pond aptly named because of the nature of the iron workings that many years ago used to be active there. This attractive stream and spring-fed pond was enlarged into a 6 acre lake by a dam at one end, and its rising waters used to drive a small wooden water-wheel and cool down the manufacturing processes involved in the small-scale production of iron. Due to economic factors, the small foundry closed many years ago and the lake was left untouched. Its waters were then used to irrigate the surrounding farmland and it became a local beauty spot where, in the summer, farm workers and their families would picnic and swim. In the cold winter months, the lake was regularly used for ice skating, with large fires lit on the ice itself. The whole village would congregate to enjoy the skating and warm themselves by the fire.

The wooden water-wheel was dismantled but the brickwork still exists today and a rather pretty waterfall, forming a small pool, remains in its place. The lake's water level is kept fairly constant due to the outlet but in times of heavy rain the lake floods in a rather spectacular fashion turning the whole length of the dam into a huge waterfall. Next to the outlet a small house was built as living accommodation for the estate woodkeeper and is still used for that purpose today.

The trees surrounding the lake were allowed to flourish and the dam end now has

An impossible dream comes true as Pete holds a brace of fours weighing 4lb 7oz and 4lb 5oz

several large oak and horse chestnut trees overhanging the water. All round the lake various weeping willows, beech and poplar trees grow in abundance, turning the lake into a sanctuary for wildlife. Recently, a small plantation of conifers has appeared on one side of the lake and several large hop fields on the other.

All these factors, coupled with huge expanses of white and yellow water lilies covering the shallow end of the lake, have turned it into one of the most beautiful settings any angler could wish for. I first heard about the lake through the match-fishing grapevine as, after a recent pollution incident, it had been stocked with a very large head of small carp and some tremendous weights were being caught. At that time one side of the lake was controlled by Tunbridge Wells Angling Club, the other side being by day-ticket. I decided to visit and fish the day-ticket side. The number of swims was very restricted and I remember longing to be on the other bank where few anglers ever seemed to fish.

I vividly recall arriving at the lake to find all the readily available swims taken so I had to resort to squeezing into the most ridiculously small gaps between trees and bushes in order to fish. I tried to join the club but was refused due to the fact that I lived too far away from Tunbridge Wells and there was a long waiting list. However, the fishing, although very crowded, was superb and I fished there many times for the carp.

Little did I (or any of the anglers) realise what was actually lurking in the murky depths of this very pretty lake. It would be true to say that perch up to 3lb had been caught in the past but so irregularly that no one I met ever mentioned them. Most anglers were fishing for the carp and everybody assumed that the recent pollution had killed all fish present at the time of the incident. Nothing could have been further from the truth and larger carp began to be caught which obviously had survived the pollution. The roach, rudd and bream populations exploded and the fishing became incredible with 100lb and 200lb plus bags commonplace. But the perch numbers mysteriously remained unnoticed and only rarely did anybody catch any.

Tunbridge Wells Angling Club lost the fishing rights they had been granted due to excessive litter annoying the local farmer. I very quickly joined the newly formed club run by the estate which now had control of the whole lake and the day-ticket system ceased. Although the cost of a season ticket was high, around £50 at the time, it was worth every penny as the fishing was so good. Even in the depths of winter, catches were still exceptional and after breaking holes in the ice, carp could be caught 'Eskimo style'.

I soon became bored with the ease of the fishing and began seeking something a little different and more interesting. At that time two other anglers had cottoned on to the small pike population present in the lake and I decided to join them and attempt to catch some of the pike. At this stage I had given up match fishing almost completely and was concentrating on the larger carp, capturing fish up to 18lb. I used very large, rock-hard boilies to try and avoid the small carp which was not always possible as I swear they used to gang up and tear the bait apart.

It was easy to switch over from carp to pike fishing, using the same tackle with the addition of a few items, and several trips were made with little success at all. The pike population appeared to be fairly small but individuals weighing up to 21lb were caught by other anglers. My fishing companion, John Bedford, and I could only manage a couple of small jacks which was extremely frustrating.

In a last-ditch attempt to improve our luck, we decided to try night fishing for the pike and during one of the first weekends, John kept getting strange twitches on one of his live-bait rods which for some time we put down to the bait struggling. Suddenly the bait roared off, very unlikely on the paternoster rig he was using. In the darkness John could not quite make out what he had hooked because he was using pike tackle but the unknown fish put up a valiant fight and John assumed that it was a small jack pike. It was difficult trying to land the fish in the pitch darkness directly under some of the big oak trees at the dam end of the lake. We chose not to use a torch in case of spooking the fish but we eventually managed to land it. On opening up the folds of the landing net the torch light revealed the most wonderful perch I had ever seen, it looked truly gigantic. Never had I laid eyes on such an impressive fish which, after we had stopped shaking with excitement, weighed 3lb 9oz. I remember saying to John that never again would we see such a wonderful fish, but little did I know what was going to happen over the next few years.

A few weeks later, with still little impression being made on the pike population, we decided to try a completely different area of the lake. Nobody fished this particular swim where two trees had fallen into the lake and the bankside area was very restricted. Overhead casting was only possible after wading out which made life unpleasant as the bottom of the lake was by no means firm and very treacherous underfoot.

The swim turned out to be where a large shoal of ever-hungry and obliging perch appeared to live. The first day John and I squeezed into the swim, and using one rod each we hooked and landed ten perch from 1½lb to 2½lb. The perch patrolled and occupied a small area under the branches of one particular tree. Any bait placed close to these branches was certain to be taken and we enjoyed many spectacular catches over the next few months.

Pete with a fantastic 4lb 13oz perch taken from a boat

We soon realised that to fish the swim too often was guaranteed to upset and split the shoal. We therefore fished it no more than once every two or three weeks, which took some doing when we were drawing a blank in other areas of the lake. This situation lasted until other anglers spotted us constantly playing fish and, as expected, they started to fish the swim. Soon anglers were fishing the swim every other day and the shoal moved on to pastures new. However, John and I had already creamed off the best perch fishing we were ever likely to find, with the only failing being that John did not beat his personal best. I managed to capture several multiple catches of 3-pounders, with the best being 3lb 8oz. John found this somewhat amusing as his best was 1oz bigger and try as I might, I could not quite beat it.

The tables were about to turn dramatically in my favour and, as a result of the angling pressure being exerted on the best swim, I began to concentrate my efforts on another neglected section of the lake. This decision was the best I'd ever made and within a short period I caught my first long-awaited 4-pounder at 4lb 6½oz. Never in my wildest dreams had I imagined how I would feel at the moment of capturing such a wondrous creature, the sheer size of which I remember until this day. I recall the struggle and then the pain inflicted on me by trying to hold up the enormous spiny dorsal fin for the trophy shot and how relieved I was to see it swim strongly away upon release.

Over the next couple of seasons I enjoyed fishing like never before, with such success never likely to be repeated and in surroundings I will find difficult to match. The main method I used during my perch fishing at Furnace Pond was live-baiting with baits either fished on free-roving or various different paternoster rigs, all somewhat based on scaled-down traditional pike-fishing ideas. It would be ridiculous to make out that the fishing was particularly difficult but nevertheless it required some thought in order to solve the different problems encountered. In all I managed to capture six tremendous perch over 4lb, with the biggest two weighing 4lb 12½oz and 4lb 13oz. My most magical capture in one day was when I landed a brace weighing 4lb 7oz and 4lb 5oz together with six others over 2lb – but that is another story for another day.

The fishing was so rewarding that even as more anglers began appearing as 'the secret Kent lake' became more widely known, I enjoyed every minute of my time there. The culmination of all my wonderful experiences at Furnace Pond was seeing the capture of the current record perch of 5lb 9oz by John Shayler, an angler I knew very well and regarded as a personal friend. John and I had spent many hours talking about the possibilities of the record being broken and I remember thinking what a nice compliment John paid me when within minutes of capturing the record fish he said that I, for my efforts, really deserved to capture the record fish and not him. On reflection I was lucky and honoured just to be *present* to witness, weigh, photograph and watch the safe release of the most incredible perch I will ever see.

Sadly, the perch fishing went into a serious decline shortly after the capture of the record fish due, I'm sure, to a number of factors but the most overwhelming one was over-fishing. I stopped fishing the lake seriously shortly before the magic and the perch began to disappear. Luckily, I have only good memories implanted in my mind of this historic water which I will always regard as 'the perch angler's Redmire'.

Never have I laid eyes on such an impressive fish

Chris Turnbull 89.

27

3
TC: The Oxford Water
Tony Miles

Back in the early years of the decade, one water above all others shone out as the Mecca for England's dedicated big-bream specialists. TC was the name by which those in the know referred to it. To the rest it remained a secret known only as the 'Oxford Water' in the constant reports in the angling press. Wherever it was, one thing was certain, the anglers who were fishing it were catching some very big bream and tench, and what's more, records were falling.

Coventry angler Tony Miles is one of our most successful and highly respected all-round, big-fish specialists and was one of the first to exploit the tremendous potential of TC. Apart from catching some very big fish himself, he was to witness and be part of what was undoubtedly one of specimen angling's high spots.

Tony is one of our most popular and prolific angling writers; he is a regular contributor to the monthly magazines, he has had several books published in the last few years and has at least one more in the pipeline.

During the summer of 1976 Trefor West and I were deeply engrossed in the tench fishing at Sywell Reservoir in the Midlands, both of us still searching for our first 6-pounder. In those days 6lb tench were still extremely rare and we were both stuck on 5lb 10oz as our personal best. Then one day we had a phone call from a mutual friend in Oxford whom we had first met during our years of carp fishing at Marlborough Pool. Martin had just had his first few sessions at a little-fished pit near his home, a water that was controlled by the Thames Conservancy. One of his first captures was a massive tench of 7lb 14oz. That was one of the biggest tench ever caught in this country and when Martin sent us a photograph of the fish, plus information that another Oxford angler, John Knowles, had landed a fish of over 8lb in weight, we realised that here was a very special water indeed. You have to bear in mind that only a handful of 6lb tench were reported to the angling press per season in those days and the record still stood at 8lb 8oz.

So little was the pit fished that the water had not even been named. It was known simply as the Thames Conservancy Pit or the TC Pit for short. I have read that the initials TC were coined as a deliberate code to hide the whereabouts of the water and to give it some ultra-cult mystique. That is simply not true. For a long time we referred to it as the Thames Conservancy water but as that was a bit of a mouthful, we reverted to the initials TC. It was as simple as that.

On 16 June 1977 Trefor and I fished TC for the first time and there were just three other anglers on the water. We immediately fell in love with this beautiful tree-lined pool and I can still remember our excitement when a huge tench rolled soon after our arrival. That first visit was totally unremarkable in terms of fish caught. We had very few bites and the fish we did catch were small. In fact, I caught one of the smallest tench I had ever seen! The next weekend, however, was to see a very different story. I was unable to fish, planning to go for a few days midweek, so Trefor went fishing on his own. On Saturday morning he had his one and only bite from a tench that he found to weigh 7lb 2oz. From that moment, TC Pit became a very important part of our lives.

The next two seasons at the water were sheer bliss as, apart from a handful of local anglers, we had the water to ourselves. The banks were still wildly overgrown with rush and sedge and the air was heavy with the scent of willow herb. Some of my most treasured memories are the countless warm, still summer nights I spent there, listening to the rats scurrying in the margins, the owls going about their grim harvest and now and again hearing the heart-stopping sound of a big fish rolling. Each morning the half light of dawn would see us hovering expectantly over the rods willing the indicators to move. Remember, this was in the days before optonics were commonplace and the rods were usually wound in at night.

There is no doubt at all that Trefor and I brought a fresh approach to TC tenching. It was the general consensus of opinion among the few anglers who fished the water regularly that because of the considered low stock density of tench, the amount of groundbait should be sparing. Most of them, in fact, used no groundbait at all, the swimfeeder being almost universally applied. Very rarely would an angler use more than a pint of maggots for a day's fishing. It was also agreed that bites were invariably finicky and a single maggot on a size 18 hook was the normal presentation. Most anglers landed a mere handful of tench per season. This general approach to the fishing made no sense to us. The evidence of our own eyes in the amount of rolling at dawn, the bubbling and the marginal activity, told us that there was at least a respectable head of fish. It followed that very light feeding would not be likely to concentrate fish

Tony's biggest TC bream
weighing 12lb 4oz

Waiting through the dawn on TC

in an area and we felt it hardly surprising that occasional tench only were caught to these tactics. We simply could not believe that the tench were finicky in a water which had received such minimal angling pressure. The bait presentation had to be at fault.

In consideration of all these facts, Trefor and I decided to be totally traditional in our approach to the fishing. We would bait heavily and accurately and fish with large baits such as lobs and flake. Right from the outset this approach was to prove its worth. Three or four tench at a sitting became commonplace, with occasional bigger catches, and the bites to our big baits were real butt-ringers. To start with we managed to keep our catches quiet but gradually information filtered out and a trickle of new faces began to appear. When I had two tremendous catches of tench in the opening week of the 1979 season, topped off by a superb 7lb 12oz specimen, the water's potential was finally exposed far and wide. Never again would we be able to fish in the idyllic solitude we had enjoyed for two seasons. The TC era of the eighties had begun.

For me, the true magic of TC Pit will always be remembered in the wonderful fishing that Trefor and I enjoyed in the summers of 1980 and 1981, and I would like to convey to you the heady atmosphere of those days. On 15 June 1980, we set up our temporary home in the swim where I had taken my 7lb 12oz fish the previous summer. It was a beautiful secluded swim, nestling as it did in the thick marginal rushes, in a small gap in the trees that flanked that bank of the pit. We set up our brolly camps side by side, mine to the left of the swim, Trefor's to the right and, even as we worked, the reeds shook in the shallow margins as tench brushed through them in preparation for their spawning rituals. Trefor swam out with the weed rake while I prepared the groundbait.

The reeds shook in the shallow margins as the tench brushed through them

Many times he swam backwards and forwards until he was satisfied that we had a clean gravel bottom on the bar on which we would be presenting our baits some 30yd from the bank. We baited heavily using over 1cwt of breadcrumbs in the week we fished, to which were added hundreds of chopped worms and flake samples.

As the light began to fade on that calm summer evening, our minds were taken off the unwelcome attentions of the myriad of insects by the sight of the first large tench dorsal, silently breaking the glossy surface over our baited area. This was followed by several more in the half light and then it was dark and time to attempt a little sleep in readiness for the onset of daybreak. I slept fitfully, as did Trefor, and long before light we had cast out our baits. The distant call of a woodpigeon heralded the dawn and then a very large tench rolled directly in front of me, the splash strangely muted by the early morning mist. At a little after 4am, my left-hand swingtip suddenly shot out straight, the rod lurched forward in the rests and the first tench of the new season battled for its freedom. That fish weighed 5½lb and was the first of over thirty tench that were caught that week. Very few were under 5lb and there were several 6-pounders and three over 7lb. The biggest was a new personal best of 7lb 13oz to Trefor.

A few weeks later there was another memorable day. I had discovered, in a very weedy corner of the pit, a clean gravel hump at about 50yd and had decided to fish it with a swimfeeder and maggots. The second rod was fishing a large lobworm in the margins alongside dense rushes. In late morning, I had a tremendous battle with a fish that had picked up the maggots, and landed a tench of 7lb 13oz, my new best. Trefor took several photographs for me before the tench was slipped back. The fish

A hard won reward – Tony Miles with an 11lb 12oz TC bream

was in superb condition apart from a very distinctive scar towards the rear of its dorsal.

After I had recast, I relaxed in my chair in a very contented mood. I was at peace with the world. At a little after midday, the drizzle stopped, the sun came out and it became a pleasant, warm afternoon. There had been no activity for some time and my eyes became heavy, following the dawn start to the day. The only sound was the drone of insects. Suddenly, and without warning, the margin fishing rod bent round savagely to the right as something shot off with the lobworm with great power. Another memorable battle ensued before the tench was safely netted. As I lifted it out, I could hardly believe my eyes. There, at the rear of the dorsal, was that scar! Just to be certain I weighed the fish again. Sure enough the scales confirmed 7lb 13oz. It must be unique for a personal-best fish to be caught twice in one day!

Trefor and I are agreed that one of our most precious angling memories is our enthralling big bream campaign at TC in the summer and autumn of 1981. When we had amassed that tench catch in June 1980, Trefor had one night hooked and lost a very large bream. Although we knew of the big bream the water contained, they had not attracted too much of our attention – we had wanted to crack the tench first. During the close season of 1981, however, we decided that our next target would be a double-figure bream and our search commenced on 16 June. We had selected an area with very little bottom weed where our planned heavy baiting programme could be used to greatest advantage. We fished that swim for four nights a week from June until October. Never before had we embarked on such an intensive campaign. As neither of us could fish the whole of each session the fishing was staggered with me fishing Thursday night until Saturday night inclusive and Trefor Friday night until Sunday.

For the first month of the season there was no sign of bream to either of us although a succession of good tench came to net. That was to change on 17 July. In the late evening, our usual thorough and accurate baiting programme completed, we settled down for yet another night session. It was a beautiful warm, breathless evening with the surface of the water mirror-smooth. Trefor and I sat well behind the rods, talking quietly, smoking and drinking endless cups of tea. As the light faded the surface became alive with the dimpling of small fry and then, in the gathering gloom, one of my bobbins suddenly shot to the butt ring and just as suddenly dropped back again. Seconds later, the second bobbin followed suit and then Trefor's indicators started.

There then followed two frustrating hours as these liners continued almost non-stop. Every minute or so, one of the bobbins would move. At a little before midnight, Trefor had a very different indication. Again the bobbin gave the initial twitch but this time, instead of dropping back again, the bobbin climbed very slowly to the butt ring. The swingtip that Trefor was using in conjunction with the bobbin pulled out straight and at that moment Trefor struck hard, stepping backwards as he did so. There then followed a few seconds of anti-climax. In the darkness, all Trefor could tell was that he had hooked something but I remember him remarking to me that it was a very feeble resistance. He was convinced he had hooked a small jack pike. The fish was played to the bank very easily indeed and when it was close in it stuck momentarily in some soft marginal weed. I turned on the small torch to sort out where the fish was and there, almost under our feet, was an enormous silver flank. Seconds later, we knelt side by side admiring our first double-figure bream. Even before the fish was weighed, we shook hands in triumph. Trefor and I had shared many memorable angling moments together but this was one of the most fulfilling.

After the fish had been weighed at 10lb 10oz and confined to our large net to await the morning, Trefor cast out again. Within minutes his other optonic sounded and once again his swingtip rose to the horizontal. This time there was no doubt that he

Chris Turnbull
89

had hooked a big bream as a ponderous weight surged to his left, fouling two other lines as it did so. The fish was played to within 20yd of the bank but then it was stalemate. Trefor could neither give nor retrieve line. Again I turned on the torch and noticed the incredible bird's nest of tangled line at the tip ring. A quick decision had to be reached to avoid the fish being lost. Quickly I bit off the fouled line, wrapping the loose end around my left arm for retrieval later. That still left the tangle at the tip but Trefor was now able to walk slowly backwards towing the fish behind him. Gingerly, I hand-lined the fish over the net and lifted it out. All the time, I had my heart in my mouth, knowing that I would probably have but one chance of netting the fish. Once on the bank, it was obvious that here we had an exceptional bream. We looked at each other in disbelief when the scales registered 12lb 10oz. What an incredible brace of fish. That bream signalled the end of the action for that night but the following night Trefor was to land a third fish of 10lb 8oz. So far I had not had a bream but I was not dismayed, my time would come.

August came and went and still there were no further signs of bream. The onset of September was greeted by a week of cold, calm and misty nights. I fished for three days and nights without the slightest sign of a bite of any description. Trefor fished a further night after I left and, in the early hours of the morning, one bite out of the blue resulted in another bream of 10lb 5oz. Would I ever catch one, I wondered?

The following Thursday afternoon I arrived to find a strong wind blowing offshore – certainly more promising conditions. A small tench was landed at 11pm and then, at about midnight, the heavens opened and the wind picked up to gale force. The camp seemed to be in imminent danger of taking off into the lake and I lay on my bedchair in the darkness listening to the torrential rain praying that I would not get a bite at that moment. With the rain still hammering down, I dropped off to sleep and was awoken with a start at about 2am by the sound of an optonic screaming. Half asleep I scrambled out of the bivvy – tripping over one of the securing pegs in the process – the pelting rain soaked my bedding in seconds. With the reel handle spinning crazily, I struck into what I first thought was a decent tench. It quickly became obvious, however, that what I had hooked was a tufted duck. To make matters worse, the tufty did a very efficient job of tangling the other line as well before I was able to release it. I will never forget how I felt that night – I could not even summon the energy to re-tackle up in the dark with the rain still pouring down. Totally brassed off, I made myself as comfortable as possible on my wet bedchair and went back to sleep. I would sort out the mess in the daylight.

The next morning dawned bright and sunny, and I was mentally prepared to start fishing again. That morning the activity from perch was intense and, after a blistering run on a large lobworm, I struck into a fish that gave me an incredible fight. I was convinced I'd hooked a good tench but was delighted when I eventually saw a very big perch in the net, a fish that weighed 3lb 1oz. TC Pit had yielded another surprise.

That afternoon the wind veered right round and was blowing very strongly inshore. Conditions could certainly have been a lot worse, but there were no indications at all on that Friday night. On the Saturday night conditions were identical until about 8pm when the wind dropped quite suddenly. By about 9pm there was not a breath of wind and it had become a very bright moonlit night. With the disappearance of the wind intense fish activity had commenced in the swim and line-bites were coming

Our next target would be a double-figure bream

35

regularly. At a little after 9pm the bobbin on the right-hand rod began to creep up, agonisingly slowly. Nine inches before the butt ring it stopped and my hand hovered over the butt in a frenzy of indecision. I resisted the almost overpowering temptation to strike and it was as well that I did for within a few seconds the bobbin started moving upwards again. As the reel commenced its slow backwind I struck into a heavy resistance that I knew immediately to be the fish I was after. Owing to an intervening bed of Canadian pondweed, I had decided to play any bream hooked high in the water, if possible. Taking the bull by the horns I put pressure on the fish to bring it to the surface and, luckily, I succeeded. Even at 40yd range I could distinctly see a great silver shape in the bright moonlight. Once it was on the surface, I kept it moving straight into the net. Stillwater bream can rarely be accused of fighting!

My feeling when that bream was lifted out in the net was pure elation and when my scales confirmed 11lb 2oz I did a victory jig around the bivvy. Anyone passing at that moment would have probably been convinced they had discovered a witches' coven! After that success the activity became even more intense with line-bites coming regularly. Another fish of 7lb came at midnight and shortly after that the sky clouded over, the wind returned and all activity ceased. The following Sunday at 11pm Trefor had the final fish of our campaign, another big one of 11lb 4oz.

Since those exciting early days, the water has been fished much more intensely by highly respected and successful specimen-hunters, people of the calibre of Alan Smith from Northampton, Alan Wilson and my old mate Phil Smith. The 83/84 season was to prove very memorable indeed. The season was not very old when Alan Smith achieved something that had certainly been on the cards for some time, a record bream of 13lb 12oz. At about that time, for health reasons, both Phil Smith and Alan Wilson were off work and able to fish full time. Several big catches of both bream and tench were to come their way during that period and the culmination was a night in September which has now become part of angling folklore. Four of us were fishing adjacent swims: Alan Smith, Alan Wilson, Phil Smith and myself. In the dark hours Alan Wilson had four bites resulting in bream of 13lb 2oz, 13lb 6oz, 13lb 8oz and 13lb 3oz. That has to be one of the most remarkable catches in angling history.

That same summer the tench were showing the first signs of wising up to baits and rigs and the catches, to traditional methods, were dropping off alarmingly. Many of us had switched to more individually concocted paste baits and for my own part I had some remarkable catches on gluten-based pastes of various flavours, fished in conjunction with bolt rigs. Others were making the first experiments by baiting heavily with carp boiled baits. Another noticeable change that year was the number of 2lb roach that were showing up accidentally and this is a pattern that has accelerated at the water until the present day when good roach are caught regularly.

In July 1984 I caught my last bream from TC, a lovely 12lb 4oz specimen, and that was the last year when the pattern of the bream fishing was as I had always known it. In June 1985, for some unknown reason, the weed distribution at TC altered dramatically so that 90 per cent of the water was very heavily weeded but a narrow strip, about 50yd wide at the canal bank, was completely devoid of bottom weed. We had established, over the years, that bream like to feed over naturally weed-free areas and it turned out that this observation was prophetically correct. Every bream in TC was concentrated in that strip of water and they became very easy to catch. The main problem of location had been solved. Several big catches of fish were taken and sadly my prediction at the time has come true. Many fish were caught by anglers who did not treat the fish with the respect they deserved and that, coupled with general angling pressures, led to many of the fish dying. Over two seasons more than twenty double-figure fish were found dead including the four biggest fish the water was known to contain. The bream fishing is now only a shadow of what it once was.

What of the future? TC is again fairly lightly fished, as the good bream days appear to be over. Big tench are still caught every season but the average size is now very small indeed. People who still fish the water tell me that a catch of tench will include many 2lb fish, unheard of in the early days when Trefor and I were making our mark there. However, an exciting development is taking place with the roach fishing. The odd big roach was always caught but in the last couple of seasons they have become much more commonplace. Last summer I heard of two confirmed catches of roach, both of six fish, all over 2lb in weight. That is roach fishing of the very highest quality and perhaps this is the direction TC specimen hunting will follow in the future. If given a chance the big bream will recover in time and I believe the stock of good carp the water contains could start to hit the headlines in the coming seasons. The same comments apply to the pike. There have always been good pike in TC, several 20-pounders having been taken. Now that there is a large stock of bite-sized tench and roach in the water, one or two of those pike could be a worthwhile quarry.

I have not fished TC Pit for the last two seasons as I have other targets to aim for and it may be that I never fish the water again. But I fervently hope that the water will continue to provide breathtaking sport for specimen-hunters for many years to come as it is a fishery that will always command a very special place in my heart.

4
Hardwick Chub

Peter Stone

Few big-fish specialists have been active longer or could boast a record of specimens to equal Peter Stone. As a man who has contributed to magazines and written books for many, many years, Peter is equally at home fishing running water or stillwater, and his enthusiasm and knowledge must rate as second to none.

One branch of angling almost entirely belonging to the eighties is stillwater chub fishing, which Peter could claim to have had a major hand in developing.

Several of the gravel pits in Peter's home county of Oxfordshire hold numbers of chub but few grew bigger than those in Hardwick. Although seemingly uncatchable, in the early and mid-eighties these impossible fish very occasionally fell to pike anglers' dead-baits. In his campaign to outwit these fabulous specimens, Peter quickly realised the value of adapting and developing this method. The ultimate reward was soon achieved, a truly massive chub, in fact, one of the biggest of all time.

Hardwick Pit is situated at Stanton Harcourt, a village in Oxfordshire, and controlled by Gerrards Cross AC. There are two lakes, one has an island in the middle with a bungalow on it in which a Mr Haines lives. Both lakes are tree lined with various kinds of rushes along the gravelly banks. Water depth varies up to a maximum of 14ft and the water is fairly clear. Caravans line one bank of the first lake with a clubhouse at one end. All in all a pleasant place to fish.

On the 'island' lake, water skiing takes place. Many times skiers have come within yards of the bank and over my lines – the main reason why I rarely fish Hardwick during the summer. While not begrudging the other man his chosen sport, fishing and water skiing just do not mix. In the second lake (the two are joined together by a small channel) sailing is popular. Although sailing does not scare fish like skiing (at least I don't think it does) upturned boats in your swim is not my idea of peaceful angling.

I first fished Hardwick in the early sixties when the appearance of some big carp caught my attention. Although I did not succeed in putting a biggie on the bank (I did nobble a 9-pounder which was probably the smallest in the lake) I did catch some nice roach of up to 1½lb and a few tench. In the early seventies I switched my attention to the big pike which had begun to show. Although I did not catch a 'twenty' I took a great number of doubles and enjoyed some very fine fishing. It was at that time I met Geoff Barnes, my now constant angling companion and one of the best mates anyone could wish for. The pike fishing remained good for several years, then deteriorated as good pike fishing usually does, and I moved on to pastures new.

In 1979 an angler told me pike anglers were experiencing runs on dead-baits which removed line from their spools at an alarming rate but which were proving impossible to hook. 'Chub', I told him and thought no more about it. In the autumn of 1980 a local angler, Kevin Pimm, fishing Hardwick for pike, caught a massive chub weighing 7lb 1oz. One Sunday morning four months later my telephone rang. 'I'm at Hardwick',

John Everard said, 'A chap has caught a 7lb chub and would like some pictures'. Another 7lb chub: I could hardly believe it. Within minutes I was on my way.

The angler was Kevin Pimm! Like his previous 'seven' the fish had picked up half a mackerel intended for pike. It weighed 7lb 4oz. Kevin had an interesting story to tell. Like other pike anglers he too had experienced very fast, unhittable runs but had connected with two. But that wasn't all. One night, before going to sleep, he wound in his bait and left it just under the rod in inches of water so the rats would not find it. In the morning some 40yd of line had been removed from his spool. Without any doubt a chub was responsible.

Now then, I'm not one who waits for others to find a good water and then barge in: I prefer to discover new waters and do the homework myself. But those reports of fast, unhittable runs and Kevin's two 7-pounders I found impossible to resist. A giant chub suddenly became a priority.

I had some experience of chub gained over many years. My father was a keen angler with pike and eels his main quarry. He was a bit of a poacher too and used to set night lines for eels which supplemented his family's diet. At the time (the late thirties) I was still at school and used to help father set and collect the lines. These were balls of thick

Peter Stone holds up his prize 7lb 4oz Hardwick chub

string with up to six hooks attached to each line. The hooks were baited with dead gudgeon. But it wasn't only eels that attached themselves to the lines – chub also found gudgeon a tasty morsel. One morning four 3lb-plus chub were on the same line, though thankfully they were only lip hooked and were released.

Between my schooldays and the early visits to Hardwick I had taken a considerable number of chub on dead fish from my local rivers and was familiar with the problems involved. One was the chub's dislike of wire, however thin, yet they were not suspicious of baits attached to thick string! A vital factor was suppleness of the hook length; thickness was unimportant (the fast unhittable runs the pike anglers were experiencing when using wire, coupled with father's night lines, had proved that).

In the sixties and seventies much of my time was spent fishing for bream and tench in gravel pits. I learnt a bit about big stillwater chub too. In another pit I often arrived at dawn to find big chub lying in the margins. But they were rarely present in daylight. I knew, therefore, that at night big chub came into the margins to feed.

The morning after photographing Kevin Pimm's big chub I arrived at Hardwick around 10am with some sprats. With a baiting needle I threaded my 6lb bs monofilament just under the skin from above the tail and out of the eye, tied on a no 6 treble (I had intended using a single but had left them at home), then pulled the treble back into the eye socket. With no lead on the line (to reduce any resistance to a taking fish) I cast the sprat as far as I could, tightened to the bait, then clipped a bobbin on the line immediately above the reel. Should a bite occur I decided I would strike immediately thus preventing the chub swallowing the bait and biting the hook off with its pharyngeal (throat) teeth.

Eight hours passed then, in the darkness, the bobbin rose. Two minutes later I was gazing down at a 6lb 6oz chub. To say it was a fantastic start would be an understatement indeed! When I went to remove the hook I discovered, to my horror, that it was out of sight – how the nylon had escaped the chub's throat teeth and had not been bitten through I shall never know. But it bore out what I had always said: chub will not (most times) swallow a dead fish attached to wire. In contrast the 'six' was not suspicious of my nylon and had swallowed the sprat on the spot instead of bolting off with it.

I went home on a high that night and resolved to spend the remainder of the season seeking my dream chub – a 7-pounder. Work commitments didn't allow as much time as I would have liked but I still managed, on average, three evenings a week. But for all my efforts just three fish picked up my baits. Two were pike, including one double which, despite being hooked inside the mouth, did not bite through the 6lb bs nylon. The third bite I tightened to but felt nothing. Worse still the hook had gone; no doubt a chub was responsible. (When a pike bites through nylon the fish is felt momentarily; with chub you feel nothing.)

In November 1981 I photographed another Hardwick 'seven'. Middlesex angler Noel Hutchinson was the lucky man. The previous week Noel and his companion, Chris Thornton, had missed several fast runs. They then recalled an article I had penned on the subject and changed to 20lb bs Dacron, resulting in Chris catching a chub weighing 7lb 2oz. Noel's chub had also been taken on 20lb bs Dacron. In *Stillwater Angling* Dick Walker wrote: 'I am well convinced that fish can always see your line however fine . . . it is the feel of it they don't like – its stiffness is unnatural. Natural filamentous things in the water are soft, not stiff.' Dick caught his 44lb carp on 12lb plaited nylon.

Noel's, Chris's and Kevin's big chub had fallen to mackerel and I reckoned the chub might become suspicious of mackerel and that a 'change bait' was needed. Although I had caught my 'six' on a sprat, before setting off the following morning, I called at a fish farm and bought some 7in rainbow trout. On arrival I attached one to an instant strike rig attached to 20lb bs Dacron and 9lb bs line and cast some 20yd. As the bait was sinking I felt a 'bonk' and released the line but nothing else occurred. On retrieving the bait I found the head almost severed, the trout otherwise unmarked. I was unlucky that morning for I'm convinced a chub was responsible.

I returned two evenings later with another 'change bait' – fresh sardines. It had been dark some two hours when the bait was picked up, I tightened and was in. Seconds later the line went slack; it had gone. But that wasn't all, the sardine from the head halfway down the flank was almost devoid of flesh. Chub – almost definitely.

Due to snow and thick ice I could not fish for three weeks but once the thaw set in I was back. One morning I arrived around 5am and made my preparations. Dawn broke shortly after and the bobbin lifted. I tightened and a big chub boiled on the surface. Then the hooks fell out: I almost cried. That evening I went back. Darkness came and an hour later the bobbin lifted and I was in. 'Thump', 'thump' on the rod top – chub. Then the line went slack. I retrieved to find the Dacron bitten through. For the second time that day I almost cried . . .

I was now fishing to a pattern. When no anglers were present (and most nights they weren't) I fished the bait (usually sardine) just beyond the rod top in 5ft of water. In the knowledge gleaned over many years of how close big chub come into the margins at night providing everything is dead quiet, I knew it was *the* place to place a bait. (Remember Kevin Pimm's experience when he left his bait in inches of water while he slept?) On the rare occasions other anglers were around I fished well out.

I arrived one evening and placed my sardine 4ft from the bank in 3ft of water. No moon was showing, I was alone and it felt right. Not wishing to scare a big chub by it spotting the rod should one venture in so close, I discarded the rod rests and instead

By the heavy thumps I knew it was something special

laid the rod on the gravel parallel to the water and pinched a piece of silver paper over the line between reel and butt ring. Once in position I knew I dare not move – it was akin to waiting for a tiger to home in on a tethered goat! Shortly after I heard a rustle; the silver paper was moving across the gravel towards the butt ring. Then it stopped. I waited but it did not move again. Five minutes later I retrieved the bait. I didn't think I had been bitten off but wanted to make sure. The bait was still intact but as I moved the sardine, the water 'humped'. I had disturbed a fish lying there.

Not very hopefully I recast (or rather dropped the sardine in), laid the rod down and clipped on the silver paper. Fifteen minutes or so later it moved again a few inches, then stopped. This time I decided not to retrieve the bait and moving very slowly I removed the silver paper, picked up the rod, tightened to the bait then put the rod across my knee, the tip pointing towards the surface, the line between my fingers. Ten minutes later the line tightened: at the same time I did likewise and the water 'humped' again. This time however I had made contact and two minutes later the chub was on the bank. The scales stopped at 6lb 2oz. On one flank was a distinctive mark which I will refer to later.

On the journey home I reflected on the evening's events. The chub had picked up my bait where, in daylight, anglers would stand to cast. My set-up was right although the Dacron hook length was still a slight worry with the possibility always present of

. . . and placed my sardine four feet from the bank

the bait being swallowed and the hook bitten off. All this meant that concentration was vital: I had to sit over the rod(s) tightening seconds after the bobbin, silver paper or line registered a bite. It was demanding fishing – the main reason why I didn't fish all night when absolute concentration would have been impossible.

The following evening found me back in the same swim. An hour into dark my sardine was picked up in the shallows almost at my feet and for the second evening in succession a chub was giving the familiar 'thump', 'thump' on the rod. As I went to remove the hook I noticed a distinctive mark on one flank – it was the same fish of the previous evening. For a big chub to make a mistake twice in twenty-four hours was remarkable and I slipped it back without bothering to weigh it.

I was now on a high and the following evening I was back again. As I walked down to the water something white caught my eye in some rushes to the right of the swim. A close inspection revealed 'my' chub now in a rigor mortis condition. What caused the fish to die is a mystery but I suspect it was stress. Two anglers I know have experienced big fish having obvious heart attacks: one was a barbel as it was being netted, the other a carp as the hook was being removed. The demise of the chub was sad but obviously the experience had proved too much. Although I spent the remainder of the season fishing, on average, three evenings a week, only pike – mostly doubles – responded and the season eventually closed.

The new season finally dawned but I did not visit Hardwick until the autumn. Until then bankside disturbance would have been intense with anglers; also water skiers would be out in force. No way, I reasoned, would a big chub venture into the margins with such activity going on. I started the new campaign in November arriving an hour before dark when I had finished work. Several chub made a mistake, all 4-pounders, good chub but not the sort I was after.

January came and I arrived one evening with an east wind blowing. It was very, very cold, one of the coldest winds I have ever fished in. I fished two rods both baited with sardines on 20lb bs Dacron and two no 6 Drennan singles. A few nights previously Pete had called round to give me the range of some new hooks. 'I'll go and catch a 7lb chub on one', I said. Many a true word . . .

It wasn't quite dark when the bobbin on the right-hand rod dropped. Two thumps on the rod top told me it was a chub and so it proved. Although a good fish (4½lb), it wasn't what I had hoped for but I didn't have time to dwell on that as two boils occurred in front of me: at the same time the bobbin on the other rod dropped. Within seconds I had picked up the rod and tightened. By the heavy thumps I knew it was something special and as I pulled it over the net my heart began beating faster. As I lifted it from the net I knew it was a 'seven'. It looked huge (well it was, I suppose!). With trembling hands I placed it on the scales. They stopped at 7lb 4oz. Months before I had decided that should I nobble a 'seven' I would get someone to weigh it so, jumping into the car, I drove into the village and phoned two friends, Dennis Moss and Pete Carpenter. When they arrived I asked them to weigh it. 'I'm not looking,' I said, 'you tell me'. '7lb 4oz' they said.

All the planning, the lonely hours spent in the darkness, the many blank sessions, finally it had all been worthwhile. I felt I had earned that chub, I really did.

I have not fished Hardwick for several years now so whether the big chub are still around I don't know. One day I will return but it will take a very exceptional fish to emulate the one which paid me a visit on that windswept night in January 1982.

5

Tring Reservoirs and That Man Wilson

An Interview with Alan Wilson

Chris Turnbull

Alan Wilson is without doubt 'specimen angling's' most prominent figure of the eighties. After a bad illness caused his premature retirement from work in 1985, he took up fishing full time. More often than not this has been on the banks of the Tring Reservoirs in Hertfordshire, waters which have long been known for their huge but difficult fish and have become even more famous since Alan took them on . . .

His enthusiasm for fishing is limitless and even the most hardened big-fish men marvel at it. Ask Joe Taylor or anyone else and they will tell you that night after night, Alan sits awake ready and watching his rods. He sleeps mostly in naps and only when he thinks his chances of a bite are minimal.

The pier at Wilstone

I went to visit Alan in his bivvy on Startops, one cold and windy day in September 1989. Talking with him made me feel like a fair-weather angler and I got the feeling that no matter how many Drennan cups he wins, he seeks no glory. He is a humble man for whom the prize money comes in handy and helps subsidise his fishing. It is his total love of fishing which drives him on and nothing can drag him away from the water's edge.

C.T.   Alan, you have been fishing Tring reservoirs for a number of years, what first brought you here?

A.W.   It's good fishing, in fact the calibre of fish you catch is unbelievable and the thing I like about these waters is you can fish them the way you want to. You're not restricted like on many waters where there's no night fishing or where you can't bait up from a dinghy or things like that, which for our kind of fishing, is detrimental in the long run.

C.T.   Do you know when the reservoirs were made?

A.W.   No, I don't actually know much about the history of them, only that there have been big fish in Tring for donkey's years, even before the war.

A joyful kiss for Alan Wilson's 12½lb ex-record tench

As long as I have my rods in, I'm happy

C.T. Yes, wasn't there even a record bream taken then?

A.W. Yes, it was taken here, from Startops. There were three big 'twelves' that were caught by somebody in the early thirties. I think his name was Fred Benchet.

C.T. How many reservoirs are there, is it four?

A.W. That's right, there's Wilstone, Marsworth, Startops and Little Tring, which is used for trout fishing.

C.T. Who are they run by?

A.W. British Waterways Board, the same as runs the canals.

C.T. Which did you start fishing when you first came to Tring?

A.W. It was Wilstone for the tench. I'd been fishing Yateley for them for a number of years. That was before the carp men got onto it. They turned up and got the tench feeding on boilies. I'm not a big lover of boilies and once the tench were onto them I wasn't so keen on fishing it, so I thought it was time for a change of venue and thought I'd have a look at Wilstone.

C.T. Were you fishing full time then?

A.W. No, I was working and living up north. My fishing here was restricted to holiday times as you could hardly come down just for weekends, especially as there was no fishing on Sundays. Anyway the first time I decided to fish it, I'd never seen it before and so came down with a mate of mine in the close season to have a look.

I remember the first time we set eyes on the water, we thought: 'What the

47

hell have we let ourselves in for'. It wasn't the size of it, it was the wall that surrounds it that was the daunting thing. You sat high up and the water's right down there.

Anyway, it wasn't too bad and we thought we wouldn't come down for the first week of the season as we expected the banks to be packed out. So we decided to come down for the second week, once the anglers had had enough and gone home, we would move in and get a good choice of where we were going to fish.

We came down on the second Saturday of the season and were surprised to find only four anglers' bivvies up. We had a wander along then stopped to talk to one of the anglers and he said 'If you want to catch tench lads, then don't fish here, fish Marsworth!'

I remember all the while we were talking, I was looking out over the water and I never saw a thing. During the hour and a half we were with him, no one was getting out of their bivvies and he said that not a lot had been caught. Me and my mate walked along the other way, along the top of the wall and where the steps are, we saw one or two fish topping right close to the wall. We peered over and could see they were bream . . . It was black with them, just like looking into a huge aquarium. My mate Jed he was fascinated with them but we walked along onto the pier and there was no one fishing it. I weighed things up and thought, 'By God, this looks nice!' For whatever reason, I took to the pier right away, I didn't know the bar was there or the submerged fence. There was just a gentle breeze coming in, so we decided to set up there.

The bream were still cleaning themselves further down, up against the wall. As we walked past carrying all the gear, we kept stopping trying to count them. It's quite a walk, like, carrying the gear with sweat running off your nose and we had to rest there for five or ten minutes. Jed came up and said he had counted over a hundred and thirty odd. I said, 'I bet you could catch some of them, perhaps with a little worm or something, on the float.' So after we finished carrying all the gear, he had a go and after about half an hour I looked round and his rod was arched round. He had one on and anyone who says that bream don't fight, don't believe them. It really gave him a scrap and weighed 10lb 2oz when he got it out. He was over the moon as it was his first double.

So he carried on and I decided to join him, then after another half hour I caught one and that also weighed over 10lb. After that, I set up my gear and having driven down overnight, I decided to get my head down.

That evening I used the dinghy to get some bait out, then Jed set up on one side of the swim and I set up on the other. We started fishing and as soon as it went dark we got line-bites. I'd never had so many line-bites in my life, the bobbins just kept going up and down all night and as soon as it came light, it stopped. We had to reel in for the rest of the day as there is no fishing on Wilstone on Sundays.

The following night, it was quite blowy and it was drizzling, then midway through it, I started getting liners again and struck a few but there was nothing there. Anyway, halfway through the night I got what I thought was another line-bite and I watched it and the bobbin never came down, so I struck and the blooming rod was nearly pulled out of my hands. It turned out to be a tench hooked fairly and squarely in the mouth and it weighed around 6lb.

Alan with an enormous 3lb 13oz battle-scarred roach

Later that day, about mid-morning I had another of just over 6lb and cast out again, then after about ten minutes, 'whap' up went the bobbin, the reel handle started spinning and I was into another of just below 6lb. Later on, while I was making my brew, my bobbin went up again. I shouted to Jed to hit it and that turned out to be just over 6lb. So that morning, our first full morning on Wilstone, we had managed to take four fish and since then it's always been very good to me, has Wilstone.

C.T.   And after that you always had a soft spot for the pier?

A.W.   Yes, as I say, I didn't know there was a bar there then or a fence but the next day a bloke came up and said, 'Have you lost any on the fence yet?' When I went out in the dinghy I found it, but as it turned out that wasn't where I was fishing. My baits were out at an angle nearer to the end of the fence, not on the top of the bar, but on the drop down and that's where I've caught them all.

C.T.   To move on a little, Alan, it was the following year wasn't it, when you gave up working to fish full time?

A.W.   Yes, it was February 1985 when I finished work. I'd taken several 6-pounders from the pier by then during my first two weeks on the water and a massive one of 9lb 6oz and that was the one that didn't half fetch some dimples in the cheeks. Then I had to go back to work.

The following season I'd had to give up work and I took up fishing full time. I couldn't get down very early because I had a hospital appointment and by the

49

time I could get down I thought there would be somebody on the pier. I came down a couple of days before the season started and had a look round but didn't look at Wilstone. I looked at Queenford but didn't fancy it. It didn't look right so I committed myself to TC. Steve Chase was there and he said I could get in beside of him. So I said I would but just had to slip into Bicester first to see Joe Taylor, to collect my Queenford ticket. When I got there, Joe said 'What are you doing? Wilstone?' I said, 'No, I'm on TC.' He told me the pier was empty and that there was nobody on Wilstone at all. Apparently Tony Chassey from the Isle of Wight had been at Joe's waiting for me and had just gone to Wilstone to try to find me. So Joe and I jumped into his van to go over.

Tony was just carrying his gear down when we found him and I told him to go onto the pier. I explained the situation, that I couldn't be there as I'd committed myself to fish with Steve on TC until Sunday and would then move over to join him on the pier. I said, 'Whatever you do, don't move off here, don't bother what anyone else is doing, you stop here and you will catch fish. I can guarantee it.'

I went back to TC and set up but after that my heart wasn't in TC really. I was just going through the motions. Sunday couldn't come quick enough. Anyway after about three days fishing I'm pretty tired like, so I reeled in the rods so I could have a good sleep. When I came to, there outside the bivvy was Tony. I looked at him, still half asleep and said, 'What the hell are you doing here?' Well it turned out that he had packed up because he said Wilstone wasn't fishing. I asked if he had caught nowt and he had caught one of 8lb 12oz. I said 'You've stopped fishing and you've had one, it weighs 8lb 12oz. What do you want, blood?'

So I decided to pack up just as it was getting light on Sunday and got over to Wilstone by half past nine and there was not a soul on it, so I went over to the pier and got settled in. That evening Tony arrived back for another week; he chose to fish the right-hand side and I took the left. Tony decided to fish worm on one and corn on the other and I put worm on one and maggot on the other. We were getting bite-offs from small pike on the worm on Sunday night and again on Monday morning, then about half past five Tony had a hellish good bite on the corn and missed it. I hadn't had a bite on maggots so put a couple of pieces of corn on one at about quarter to six. At about ten past six I got this bite and struck. I'd got a good fish on and had got so used to being bitten off by pike that I expected it again but after playing it for at least a quarter of an hour, we caught a glimpse of it a couple of times and it looked like a decent tench. It kept running backwards and forwards but gradually I worked it round so it was in one corner away from the fence.

C.T. Were you using quite a light line?

A.W. No, no, I was geared up for keeping them out of the fence, 8lb main line. I played this fish around and Tony was down at the bottom of the wall waiting with the net. The fish was coming in on its side and I thought it looked like a decent fish. I'll never forget it, because when I drew it over the net, Tony lifted a bit early really and for a split second it was balancing on the rim and I wasn't sure which way it was going to fall, but it slipped the right way, into the net. Tony said: 'By heck we've got something here.' We carried it around in the net to the grass and I went to hunt in my bag for the scales and weigh sling. While

A tremendous fish

I'm searching for them, Tony keeps saying 'My word, we've got something special here.' So once I'd done the usual procedure, wetting the sling and zeroing the scales, we put it in the sling. I stood with the scales and he put the fish on so I could lift it in front of him. He said: 'Your scales are wrong.' But I thought they were okay. So he told me to put it down and then lift it steady. So I did and as I lifted, he went: '7, 8, 9, 10, 11' and I thought: 'What the bloody hell is he on about?' Then he went: '12' and I thought 'When's he going to stop?' So anyway he decided it was just a touch over 12½lb. Well, I thought he was kidding so I had a go at reading the scales and it weighed the same, so then I got it out to have a look and thought, 'Bloody hell, it is a big fish.' Then it dawned on me that it was a new record. It annihilated the other one, the one before that.

C.T. That's right. What was the record then, can you remember?

A.W. Well, the record was about 10lb 1oz wasn't it? Tony Chester caught it here and then Joe De-arville had one of about 10lb 10oz I think, and it had bettered that by nearly 2lb.

C.T. When did you start fishing Startops for the roach?

A.W. In September 1985. I had a lot of 'twos' and my first 'three' at 3lb 2oz.

C.T. And by then were you fishing full time?

A.W. Yes, I'd been on Queenford but had blanked and thought 'Well, that's enough of that', so I came here to Startops for the roach.

C.T.   So how many over 2lb did you have that first year?

A.W.   Nineteen up to 3lb 2oz, in about five weeks' fishing. I had one brace in the same night weighing 3lb 2oz and 2lb 15oz. It was a rough night, raining hard and blowing, one of those nights when you hope nothing happens because you don't want to get out of the bivvy. But it was worth it. It was early as well, it started about half past seven and I'd caught the big one by twenty past eight then about half past one in the morning I got another bite and had the 2lb 15oz – 6lb 1oz for two fish, that's something that is.

C.T.   Was it the following year you went back to Wilstone and had some more doubles?

A.W.   No, this was 1986, I started there on the pier with Phil Smith but it came over very hot and the tench in Wilstone don't like it hot, they feed best in overcast conditions. I had one bite in a fortnight and got a small one of 5lb 12oz. I couldn't get a bite anywhere the start of that season. I went over to Queenford and blanked there apart from another small tench, then I came over to Startops in the end of July. I fished it for a while and didn't do too good until the bream went bananas but the roach didn't show. I only had one small one of 1lb 12oz in the middle of the afternoon. I thought if the bream are feeding here, they might be feeding in Queenford so I went back over there and had another blank.

Just before Bank Holiday Monday, I thought I'd have two or three days on Wilstone before I had to go back home to Blackpool to see my doctor. On the Sunday I went there with a gallon of maggots because these tench are supposed to feed well in mid-July to August and if you can just hit it right you can have a good do, like. I put my markers out and baited up then waited through till Tuesday and never had a bite. On the Tuesday I was watching the bream over in the distance, they had been rolling for two days. So I thought tonight I'll put the markers out a bit further and see if I can catch a bream. I had a trial cast to see how far I could whop it out and I was getting about 70yd, so I moved the markers out and baited up and sat through Tuesday night and never had a bite.

About 6 o'clock though on Wednesday morning the indicator dropped like a stone. I struck and played this fish and it turned out to be a tench of 5lb 11oz. I cast out again and then re-cast the other rod and was putting on the indicator when the first one flew up. I struck and was into a smaller fish which turned out to be a perch of 2lb 8oz. From then on the indicators never stopped, it was just like World War III. It was like that from six in the morning to nine at night. As fast as you could throw them in, they were biting. I've never known fishing like it in my life and if I'd landed all the fish that had given me bites that day, it would have been the best catch of tench that anyone had caught in their life. I finished up with sixteen and a perch with the best one being 8lb 7oz.

The next night I had a bream of 11lb 4oz and the following day another fourteen tench up to 8lb 14oz, so that's how Wilstone can fish.

C.T.   Was that from the pier again?

A.W.   No, that was from the wall at the top of the car park. After that I had to go to see the doctor back home in Blackpool. While I was away Steve Scales took some more fish from that swim including the one that I'd had at 12½lb the year before, he caught it at 10½lb.

C.T.   You then had a few more tench from Wilstone up to over 8lb and some more bream from Startops. Let's move on to 1987.

A.W. Well, I started that season again on the pier and had a hell of a start. The first fish weighed 9lb 10oz, just the one, on the opening day. Over the next six days, I finished up with about thirty-odd altogether.

After another stint on Queenford when I had my first bream out from there, one of 12lb 2oz and then at the end of July we came on here (Startops) and started catching roach. The year before nobody had caught any roach and they were all saying they had all died because they have got this disease columnaris. But I'd said: 'Rubbish, there's still plenty of roach in here,' and then, for whatever reason, they started turning up again in 1987. We had some nice bream as well. I had three 'threes' that year, with the biggest weighing 3lb 3oz.

C.T. So how many 'threes' have you had out of here altogether?

A.W. I've had ten now, two of them last week.

C.T. Let's move on to 1988.

A.W. That was another incredible year at the opening. Not many tench but what I had were very good fish. I had a 9lb 8oz on opening day and then nothing till a couple of days into the season. It was quite laughable, because I'd always been saying that none of these tench feed in the dark in Wilstone. Funnily enough I'd caught my first tench ever from the water in the dark, that was the only one till the start of '88, all the rest were caught in the daylight.

The 9lb 8oz came at mid-morning, out of the blue. I'd said to my mate Bob that they don't bite in the dark here and at about ten past one in the morning I got this bite and it was just like a carp bite, the bobbin flew up and the reel

'By heck, we've got something here!'

started churning just like a blur. I didn't need to strike and just leant into it. Then it nearly wrenched the rod out of my hands. I managed to control it and got it round, then netted it and weighed it at 10lb 13oz. The following morning at about 5 o'clock, I got another one out which was exactly 10lb. They were twenty-seven hours apart and I think that one day somebody will catch two doubles out of here in the same day.

After a day or two I had a 9lb 6oz and a small one of 5lb 12oz, then on the 10th July I had an 8lb 10oz. I did a month from 16th June to 16th July and had six fish, but they were very good fish.

I went from there to Queenford for three weeks and had my best bream ever of 15lb 5oz. Then I came back to Startops and started catching roach again. 2lb 10oz was the first one, then two bream, after which the swim went dead. In the next swim, I had a few bream and roach, then that spot went dead, so I moved again to where we are sat at the present (Piggeries Bank).

I started to get it together a bit there, I'd had a few and then it started to go dead on me. In the meantime Joe came down to do a bit of fishing with me. I was fishing straight out, where my markers are now, at above 12 o'clock say. I said to Joe: 'I'm going to move.' He said: 'What, you're going to move again?' I replied: 'Well, I'm not going to move my bivvy, just the position I'm going to fish. I'm going to move round to just about ten to twelve.' 'Why?' said he 'What's that for?' I told him: 'It's just a theory I've got, where I'm fishing now is where I've raked, I'm fishing on silt. If I cast to about ten to, I'll be fishing on top of the weed, which is dying down now.' So I put some fresh markers out about 5–6yd further out and baited with fresh bread and casters. On the first night I had one of 2lb 8oz and the second night I got a 2lb 12oz, 2lb 11oz and 3lb 4oz. After that I blanked a night, then had a 3lb 13oz on the Friday night.

C.T. What, that's two 'threes' in the same day?

A.W. Well, I suppose it is in retrospect, but my days run into one another and I think of them being from when I go out to bait up after tea, till I do it again the following day. In fact I had three 'threes' following one another.

C.T. And the 3lb 13oz is the third biggest roach ever caught, isn't it?

A.W. Well, so they say. I don't know. There may be other bigger ones that have never been reported. But the *Angling Times* reckons it is.

C.T. A tremendous fish.

A.W. It was. We set off fishing for 'threes' and I wondered how big they can get. We discussed these things with the lads on the bank and I said 3lb 6oz to 3½lb. They have got that columnaris and I thought by the time the roach reach that weight they are getting old and they must be on their way out, especially as eventually the disease kills them. But then I had the 3lb 13oz, so you have to re-evaluate it after catching that.

Since then, another thing has come to light when Steve Scales came down to fish a weekend with me. He caught a roach of 3lb 7oz, the second best to come out. Steve recognised it as the one that Calvin had the year before. It had an orange patch like a birthmark on its cheek. Calvin caught it at 3lb 1oz so that's 6oz growth in a year. I'd like to think that my 3lb 13oz could put on a further 6oz since I last had it, then I can catch it again.

C.T. Alan, I'm amazed that you manage to keep your enthusiasm going day after day, summer and winter, year after year.

A.W. Oh well, I've been fishing forty-odd years now, Chris.

C.T. But full time, that's another ball game isn't it?

A.W. Yes, well you know I've always said the day I'm fed up with fishing they will be carrying me away in a wooden box. As long as I have my rods in, I'm happy.

C.T. Even through the blanks.

A.W. The blanks don't bother me at all. It gets to some people I know, if they haven't had a fish for several days. You can understand it, if you've only got limited time but as far as I'm concerned time doesn't matter, it's on my side, it's immaterial.

A fantastic brace of
Startops roach weighing
3lb 2oz and 2lb 15oz

6

Wensum Giant

John Bailey

Norfolk's River Wensum had for many years enjoyed a reputation as an extraordinary roach fishery. In the seventies its big-roach fishing peaked in a way previously unprecedented on any river, a peak which unfortunately tailed off into one of angling's most tragic declines. By the mid-eighties the roach had almost totally vanished from the river; the few remaining ones, however, had become massive. Few anglers knew the river well enough to fish for them, but for those who did, the rewards could be enormous.

John Bailey had long been recognised as an expert on Wensum roach and had caught a huge number of 2 and 3lb specimens from its reaches. Here he tells the story of a campaign to catch a giant which would top them all and how he duly landed one of the biggest river roach of all time.

John is a tremendously successful all-round angler with very big fish of all species to his credit. He is probably also the country's most prolific angling writer, who apart from regularly contributing to weekly and monthly publications has written and edited many very popular books.

There is little doubt that Norfolk's River Wensum battles it out with the Hampshire Avon for the title of the greatest English roach river of all time. What is sure is that over the years the Wensum has outclassed all its other East Anglian rivals in both numbers and size of fish. In size of roach, too, the Wensum also certainly ousts the Dorset Stour even if it does not have the long-recorded history of that river and her sister the Avon. The Wensum is more remote in mid-Norfolk and until the fifties was relatively unknown outside the county even though numbers of large roach were being taken long before then.

What is also true is that without its history of roach and, latterly, barbel, the Wensum would not be the nationally famous river it is today. It is not a very long water and loses its identity at Norwich where it merges with the Yare. Nor is it a spectacular river running as it does through a wide, flat, often dreary, flood plain. The frequent mills do provide some water variety and some scenic attraction but, for the most part, the river is quite unremarkable. This is especially so due to the more recent works of the Inland Drainage Board; the banks are left free of all obstructions and not even willows are allowed to droop as of old. Constant dredging has led to a relatively uniform bottom and in places the course has become quite canalised. All in all, then, not the river dreams are made of were it not for the mystery of misty dusks and, of course, those still remaining, few, massive roach.

Wensum roach really are something to behold. They are the deepest shouldered, most powerful looking fish I have ever come across. Their colouration is equally vivid and even their fight is often bold and dashing. Clearly, the cool spring waters of this

Upper River Wensum from Guist to Attlebridge (the big roach reaches)

56

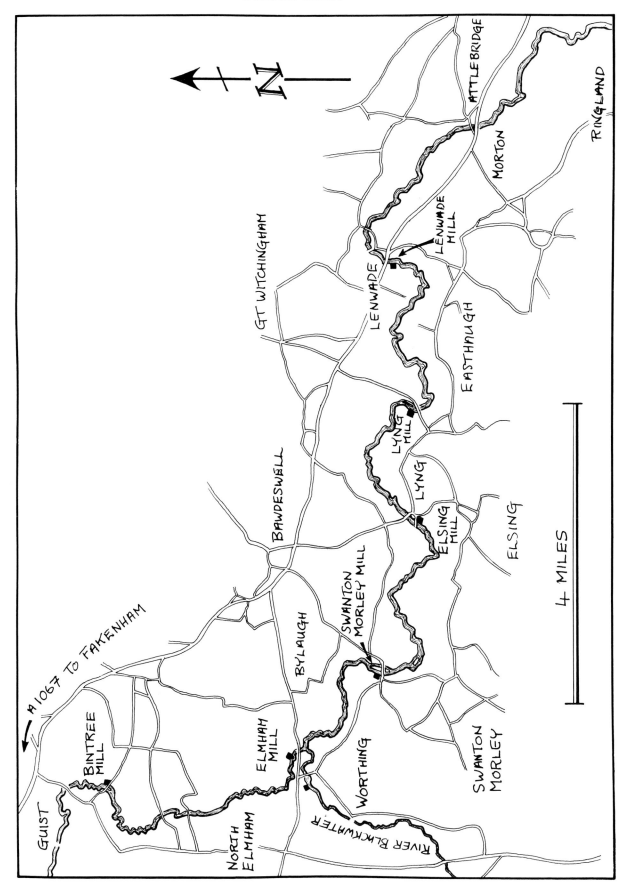

Bintree Mill on the River Wensum

essentially chalk river suit them well. There is plenty of food for the young fish but, more importantly, there are massive amounts of snails, shrimps and general crustaceans to feed the roach of 12oz plus. Growth thereafter becomes rapid and 2lb fish are not infrequently only seven years old. Scale readings have proved fish of 2lb 10oz–2lb 12oz as only eight years old and as growth can continue until the tenth or eleventh year the potential of the Wensum roach is extraordinary. Indeed, the potential has, of course, been fulfilled over and over in the past with hundreds of 2lb fish and nearly a dozen, fabulous, 3lb roach.

Before we talk of the eighties, the past of the Wensum must be covered, at least to some extent, if we are to understand how these superfish came into existence. The thirty-odd years between the mid-fifties and the present day can be divided into distinct periods: 1955–67 was a period of plenty; in the late sixties to the turn of 1970, roach stocks were badly hit by the disease columnaris; 1972 to 1977 witnessed the most famous Wensum boomtime of large fish up to slightly over 3lb; from 1978 to the present day, the numbers of roach have declined dramatically but, at the same time, the average size has unbelievably increased. By the mid-eighties, the era of the superfish on the Wensum had finally arrived. For those hardy and dogged enough to stick with the river, the ultimate rewards were mind-blowing.

I did not personally know the river between 1950 and the columnaris outbreak but I

The 1955–67 period was a time of plenty

have heard stories of it. Simply, it must have offered the most incredible roach fishing ever known to Man. From reports, it hardly mattered where you sat, you were on roach. The only need ever to move was to go in search of bigger fish when one was tired of pounders. Hundred-pound bags were commonplace. The match king, Ivan Marks, commented that the roach would have eaten his hat had it fallen in. Jack Fitt, now manager of the Norfolk flyfishers, caught twenty-six roach over 2lb in a single sitting. Double-hook rigs were commonly used and a pair of roach of 5lb was once recorded. One shoal of roach at Lyng was accurately measured to stretch, bank to bank, for 700yd. On one of the local club matches in 1958, 80 per cent of the anglers weighed in over 40lb of roach. A 2lb 13oz roach was even caught on dry fly in 1962. Otters flourished all along the more remote upper valley and the pike waxed fat; the decade records many 20-pounders and not a few 'thirties'. In all probability the Wensum had offered roach fishing of this quality for decades before 1950 but unfortunately it was not to continue.

From around 1967 the deadly roach disease columnaris began to infect the river. The symptoms were at once obvious: red-raw ulcers appeared all over the fish's flanks; one or more fins were frequently eaten away; blindness became common; the balance of the fish became impaired and a great number of the roach began to die. It is probable that 90 per cent of the roach stocks perished. Vast rafts of bodies moved slowly to the sea. At times the mill sluices became clogged and the valley was massed with herons and gulls. By 1970, quite obviously, the colossal bags of the previous years were over and the river was rarely fished. When I started on it around that time other anglers were rare; in fact, almost invariably I was alone.

It took me time to get to know the Wensum but by 1972 I was coming to grips with it and realising that the fishing was still remarkably worthwhile. True, in most places, the numbers of roach were badly down, but to compensate, the average size was generally up. I do not say I never caught smaller roach – once in 1974 I landed nearly two hundred in a day – but between 1972 and 1977 more fish came out over 2lb than under. As the period progressed the average rose even higher until, in the latter days, fish of less than 2lb 10oz were infrequent.

Many of these roach were columnaris survivors. My first 'super' roach of 2lb 13oz had recovered but still bore the horrifying scars of the disease. Without dorsal fin and still bearing sores, it was not a pretty fish even if a large one. In fact, most of the fish showed some signs of past suffering even if, in many cases, just scales were missing or rather jumbled and rearranged. Despite this the roach of that period were still dynamic fish and well worth catching. A great many of us lived for them in those days. John Wilson was a wizard with a float and a centre pin. That was his style and though I do not believe it to be the method for the very largest fish, he had several of whiskers under 3lb. Another float man was the talented and dedicated Jimmy Sapey who, in a blistering fifteen minutes, once landed three roach for, I think, just 6oz under 9lb! Jimmy Henry, Terry Houseago, Perry King, Martyn Page, Joe Reed and several others also were on the river enjoying sensational big-roach fishing.

Of course, it was not now as easy as it once had been. The roach were fewer, old, wary and had a tremendous amount of natural food available to them. Even in the peak years of 1973 and 1975 blanks were all too frequent. Indeed, in December 1975, I recorded thirty-one blanks in succession . . . yes, we all worked for our fish but, of course, the results were well worth the effort for the big-fish men in those days of dedication.

Possibly the biggest river roach ever – John Bailey smiles over his 3lb 10oz Wensum roach

By the 1976–77 season, it was apparent that roach were, in the main, becoming fewer. Not every swim could be relied upon. During the dawns, the prime time to see fish, rolling roach were now comparatively rare. We were still there on the Wensum, still catching roach but we knew a decline had set in. Between 1978 and 1980–81 this knowledge was reinforced. The days of 40 and 50 2-pounders in a season were over: now it was a case of a handful of fish containing exceptional specimens. There were a few areas that proved an exception to this general rule – Bintree Mill for instance – where the catches held up well as late as 1983. Over the river as a whole, all of us struggled and many like Joe Reed and Terry Houseago gave up the river for lost. The only signs of any promise were a scattering of young, immaculate, fast-growing roach. By 1981–2 some of these roach had reached around 2–2½lb and were probably – though incredibly – the results of the 1975 and 1976 summers and the semi-successful spawning of those years. From the March of 1982, I myself ducked out of the fanatical roaching I had pursued for a dozen years. I felt due a rest from this gruelling river and a move onto other pastures and species.

Between 1982 and 1984 I did little more than keep a casual eye on the river. Occasional visits produced little, though knowledge of a pre-spawning gathering ground gave me three 2-pounders in three casts in late winter 1984. Not until the late summer of 1985 did I take serious interest in the Wensum once more and then I cannot pretend the impetus was mine specifically. Rather, for a couple of years I had

'A bloody chub, Roger, after all that'

been partnered by Suffolk man Roger Miller. We had concentrated on pike, bream, tench, rudd and carp even, but now he pressed me for an introduction to the Wensum. One Friday evening in late August and in mellow heat the two of us walked the four most productive miles of the great days. It was, as you can guess, a walk of heart-rending nostalgia; at every bend, under every alder, along every straight a memory sprang to my mind. Here in the shadows I imagined Terry Houseago's crouching figure; there in the sunset I could picture Joe Reed's tall blond figure stalking to his swim for dusk. The river outwardly had hardly changed. Certainly the last dredging had taken place in 1975–6 and the banks looked well matured. It was when, towards the middle of the stretch, we found one of my long-lost rod rests poking through the marsh grass that I felt truly moved for what I believed I had lost.

I remember Roger and I paused at that point and sat on our Barbours looking this way and that, up and down the river. Very seriously Roger asked me if I believed this stretch worth fishing once more. I shrugged, I simply did not know. All I could point to were the mint 2lb plus fish of two or three years back and suggest that they were few in number, they would be ten years old by now. If nature had been kind, I suggested, and they had survived, they could be very large fish indeed. Roger that evening pushed and pushed for a commitment as we walked the river homewards. The water, though, was quite dead as far as the eye could see and I hesitated until the very point of closing time. Then, walking out in the car park, I agreed to give the Wensum the winter through. I need hardly tell you that I drove up the valley side with a sinking heart. The prospect of the after-work dashes, the long weary walks, the wet, the cold, the vagaries of the river levels and speeds, the problems of dead weed and the clearest certain knowledge of the scarcity of the roach did little to cheer me. The job we had set ourselves, I knew, would be a long and hard one – possibly for precious little reward.

We met the following day on the river and talked the coming campaign over very carefully. I made the difficulties quite clear and stressed that, now the quest had begun, it demanded total commitment. I need not have worried on that score; Roger would go on to fish that river as if his very life depended on it. His obsession was on the way up and his enthusiasm matched mine every step of the journey. We decided to use bread as bait. All through the seventies it had been my favourite, firmly legered in large pieces on size 8 and 10 hooks to 3lb line. We would use butt indicators when we could and only when the current was too strong would we go onto quivertips. These were the tactics that had served me well in the past and landed well over three hundred 2-pounders for me. It was hardly surprising that we should stick with them. I really believed that flake attracted the biggest roach and, of course, as most of our fishing would be done at night, it was only sense to leger. All this was very traditional stuff; it will surprise no one. Where we did progress from the seventies a little was in our approach to prebaiting.

Remember, we started the campaign in the late summer when the river was still gin clear. This decided us to prebait many different swims heavily and watch the results from the bank. Our nights took a predictable routine. Beginning at the head of the stretch we walked from one prebaited swim to the next. In each we looked intently for signs of the bread having disappeared. Where it had, a further four to six slices of bread

63

were made into pellets which were evenly scattered on the river bed. If the bread remained from the previous evening, we did not introduce any more but left the swim until the next night's checking. In this way we worked down the entire four miles until we reached our second car, piled in and drove back to the first car parked at the head of the stretch. At that point we refrained from fishing. We did not wish to risk scaring roach that might just be building up a taste for our bread. What we were preparing was the most elaborate, long-term ambush.

Of course, it did worry us that in those swims where bread was disappearing roach were not the culprits. Thieving chub were a possibility as pioneers had settled in the stretch and had bred. Swans were ruled out as the swims' beds were generally far too deep for them. This still left any amount of diving ducks that the valley attracted in at night. Of particular concern was the frequent arrival of tufted ducks as dusk fell. After a couple of weeks some four swims began to look very promising. Each evening we found all, or most, of the previous night's bread gone. So great was the feeding activity in these swims that the bottom algae weed was being scraped clear and a clean shiny sand bottom was appearing. The question remained though: were the nocturnal feeders fish or fowl?

We approached the full moon. Roger sat on one swim and I on the next. We adjourned at 11pm and neither of us reported any bird activity. The following day the bread had gone when we arrived to inspect at dawn. That evening we sat up on the third and fourth swims. No disturbance. At dawn, the bread there, too, had disappeared. The time had come to fish. Confidence ran high.

Our first session was on a bright, warm, September night. We were on a bend quite large enough for the both of us to fish in comfort and after baiting all the four swims, we settled in and prepared, if necessary, to fish the night through. It was bliss to be on the Wensum seriously again after the break of years; I had forgotten how much I missed the bleakness of the valley, the sound of the owls and the far-off barking of the foxes in the pheasant woods. We sat well back, not talking at all and in the silence my memory flickered over past nights when the bobbin had jumped and thudded to the butt. It was heady to be back.

If I remember rightly nothing happened until 10pm, some two or more hours after darkness. Roger had a line-bite and immediately afterwards my bobbin jumped. There were absolutely no birds on the water and we were wound tight as coiled springs. Roger's bobbin was the next to go . . . right to the rod. He struck. He was in. The water splashed in silver fragments. I had the net to hand and the torch ready by my side. Roger though was cursing. He could feel on his rod what I could see in the beam. A chub. A blasted slobber-chops chub spewing out our bread as it lay there gasping on the grass. That moment we were near despair. We packed at once and sat miserable men in the pub. Glass by glass the horror subsided to a dull ache. Chub, we had always known, were a possibility along the stretch. We had taken a knock, but far from a fatal one. We were hardly past the first bell . . .

The following two weeks saw our nights spent continually on all four 'going' swims. We reported no bird activity at all and quite a few blanks. Almost worse than the blanks were the chub, six in all, up to 5lb 4oz. To us, then, they were horrible fish and almost enough to break our proud roaching spirit. But, of course, we kept at it: putting in the bread and fishing on, night after gentle autumn night. The weather remained kindly and dry so the Wensum continued low and clear. We would see the scheme to some sort of conclusion. Of course, contingency plans were being drawn up. One was particularly simple. If the roach would not come to us, then we would have to go to them. The tactic had been relatively successful ten years back and I was willing to give it a new whirl now. Anything that would put roach on our bank was worth a trial.

As a result, on one October Sunday, Roger and I met early in the day two miles above our first chosen swim. Hour by hour, well into the darkness, we worked every yard of the water. We were still half a mile above swim 1, quite totally knackered and without a single bite to either rod. There was a steady drizzle and the night was turning cold. I, I admit it, was all for a return to the car and a drive to the nearest warm fireside. It was Roger who urged us on to the top swim when just the thought of yet another hour filled me with loathing.

We settled down as we had done a score of times before, our baits only a yard apart and two beams directed at the ghostly white quivertips. It was a blustery night and the breeze continually caught at the lines and plucked at the slender glowing wands. Cold began to grow deep, the way it does when you have been warm and walking and then simply sitting out in the damp. Some forty minutes into the session, the tip knocked. I tensed. Either the fish had left the bait or it was lying there with it between the lips, savouring it, turning it around, preparing for a swallow. And so it was! The quivertip left the torch beam entirely and the whole rod was on the lurch when I grasped it. Such a bite could only be from a chub and I knew it when I felt that pulsing, heavy, first run. I was distraught. 'Chub,' I cried. 'A bloody chub, Roger, after all that.'

I simply hauled that fish back up the swim and powered it to the surface. Roger had

It was a fish that defied my imagination

the torch on the water and the light caught the swirl. For a second the fish was illuminated. There was no mistaking the back, dorsal and tail of a huge fish . . . a roach! The bend went out of my rod. I threatened to freeze but Roger kept me at it. Now I was playing the fish carefully feeling its every wallow and head shake with mounting terror. A minute passed. Then two. The roach was rolling now, hard up, gasping the night air. 'The net, Roger, it's ready.' No reply. 'Christ's sake, Roger, net it,' I screamed. A calm reply: 'We left the net half a mile upriver. I remembered it an hour ago. Just keep it coming in. Towards my hands here in the water. I'll catch it when it beaches!' With no other option, I kept the roach on its side, on its way to the wicket keeper: a sweep of the hands, a swathe of flying silver and there on the golden sedge lay my roach.

I tell you we fell on the damn great thing where it lay and rejoiced. Our whoops filled the valley as we weighed it once, twice, three times. Perhaps it was a shade under, perhaps it was barely, but since we have settled for 3lb 10oz. It was massive. It was pristine. It was the most magnificent roach I had ever beheld. It was a fish that defied my imagination and we looked carefully for any signs of the hybrid about it. Nothing. Every check indicated a huge, true, roach. We took our photographs, had a last look at the silver and crimson leviathan and returned it to the depths.

Postscript

The campaign did not end there. Further roach were caught: a 3lb 5oz roach to me and a 3lb 3oz fish to Roger were the two succeeding highlights. Since 1986, however, I have not been back. Spectacular as these results were, in the entire winter we only landed five roach. A man has to live as well as to fish.

Over and over, however, I have pondered the problems of the Wensum in my mind. For years we all believed that columnaris had induced infertility in the survivors: wrong. Then we believed that pollution had dealt a death blow: not the whole answer. Next we blamed agricultural run-offs and high nitrate levels for killing young fish: almost certainly incorrect. Now we are sure that the dredging of the seventies produced a river of fast water run-offs – so rapid in fact, that roach yearlings cannot fight the current or find shelter. As a result they are swept to their deaths through mill after mill. Only larger fish can survive and though they have spawned several times the vast majority of their progeny face inevitable winter displacement and death.

Anglian Water Fisheries staff now agree. Sympathetic dredging is being urged on the Inland Drainage Board. Fallen trees, for example, are being allowed to remain to provide shelter from the winter pushes. Perhaps we will be in time. Perhaps those few big fish have survived, will spawn again and again and the rebirth will take hold. It is just possible that in the nineties, the Wensum will live again and once more Joe Reed and Terry Houseago will patrol the marshes at dusk and dawn.

7
Yateley Carp
Chris Ball

Out to the west of London lie vast complexes of flooded gravel extraction workings, many of which have achieved fame as carp fisheries. Near the village of Yateley one group of pits has stood out as remarkable for regularly producing some truly colossal fish. One in particular, a 45lb mirror carp, really put these waters on the map, making no book on big-fish waters complete without their inclusion.

Chris Ball, a well respected and highly successful carp angler has lived near to and fished the Yateley complex for many years. His knowledge of these waters and the fish that inhabit them goes right back to the days when Yateley was the well kept secret of just a few specimen carp hunters. Few anglers have been able to watch these fisheries grow in status as closely as Chris or would be more qualified to tell its story.

The North Lake

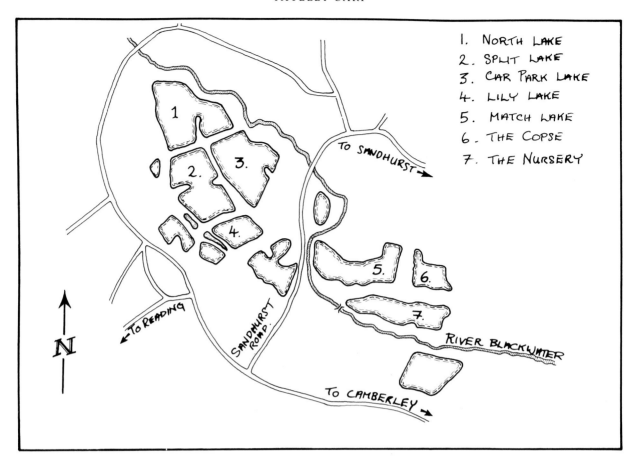

1. NORTH LAKE
2. SPLIT LAKE
3. CAR PARK LAKE
4. LILY LAKE
5. MATCH LAKE
6. THE COPSE
7. THE NURSERY

The Yateley complex

There can be little doubt that with the massive rise of carp fishing in recent years Yateley holds a firm place, and is a complex of waters that has truly come of age during the last decade. For this is a modern story of carp fishing. The lakes at Yateley have never seen a piece of flake, worm or even the humble potato cast into their depths to tempt a carp. For Yateley was born of the boilie, particles and hair-rig age.

Like so many gravel pits that abound in the South of England, these lakes came into existence when sand and gravel were in great demand for the huge building programme that Britain undertook. The deposits were large for, by the time the diggers had left, nearly 80 acres of land were flooded making fifteen or so different lakes of various shapes and sizes. Fish were present but I can trace no carp stockings until much later and very few people had the opportunity to even cast a line, for fishing on a regular basis did not take place until the early seventies. The Ready Mix Concrete Company at this time instigated an angling club under the name of Halls Angling Scheme (HAS). They had some good waters throughout the country some of which were known for carp, such as the big lake at Darenth.

The carp stockings at Yateley came at several different times mainly at the instigation of Ken Suter who was then angling manager. The stocking records of HAS are very poor and today there is no written evidence of what actually happened. My information is gleaned from many sources who remember what happened at Yateley. I can trace three definite stockings of carp that took place in the mid- to late sixties:

1.   Six or seven carp were brought from Sutton-at-Hone in Kent and placed in the North Lake. They languished there for ten years uncaught and unnoticed; one of these fish was destined for great things by the time the eighties arrived.
2.   The Match Lake received two hundred carp of 1½–2lb during 1968. Ken Suter wanted to create another carp water like Darenth. Work conducted by Dr Anne Powell of the London Polytechnic showed that the growth rate potential at Yateley was two and a half times the average for all species present and Ken knew he was on to a winner.
3.   The lakes to the east of the complex namely the Copse and the Nursery were originally leased by Alec Holmwood who owned the adjacent Tri-lakes fisheries. In 1965 his son Colin took over the business. It was Colin who stocked the Copse, Nursery and Tri-lakes with carp in 1967. This amounted to 100 carp up to 10–12lb. These fish were purchased from Weirwood Reservoir. In 1969 Tri-lakes relinquished its lease and these two waters were put under the Halls Angling Scheme as a part of the Yateley Complex.

Chris Ball with a 21lb 12oz Yateley Match Lake mirror carp

Yet another Yateley 'thirty' for Richie McDonald, this one at 30lb 10oz

These various stockings of carp have now, in the last decade, made Yateley so famous for big fish. But in the early seventies hardly anyone pursued these fish, for Yateley was classified as a good general fishery and in fact the North Lake came to be known for its outstanding large tench. One or two people, of course, did catch carp and I remember that Peter Springate was given a chance to fish the Match Lake before it went on ticket and he caught a 15½lb mirror in 1973. This showed that the carp were growing well, not surprisingly, with no real competition for food with other species. But the Match Lake did suffer at the hands of Ken Suter's replacement John Newby who wanted to turn this lake into a match-fishing lake. He unfortunately didn't bother to check what had been stocked in there or even that it was really intended to be a carp lake. He put a tremendous amount of roach, bream, tench, etc into the Match Lake over a period of time. This without a doubt had a detrimental effect on the carp and stopped these fish ultimately reaching 30lb some time ago.

As the pace quickened in carp fishing in the mid-seventies so a local group of anglers who were part of the Reading Specimen Group began to explore Yateley and, in particular, the Match Lake for they had heard reports of good-sized carp being spotted cruising around. They were good anglers and armed with sweetcorn and allowed to fish at night they soon had the Match Lake fish under their spell. During the 1977–78 season they accounted for a good percentage of carp with quite a few over 20lb. All these were mirrors; the commons, even to this day, never seemed to grow into big fish. It might have been Micky Bond who landed the first 20lb plus Match Lake fish in 1977. They kept all this pretty hush hush for they knew they were on to a good thing for later in 1978 they caught a fish of over 25lb which was pretty good going in those days.

Richie's Yateley monster

Chris Turnbull 89.

In tandem with these developments Yateley's North Lake was receiving consider-able attention from the specialist tench boys. These included Phil Smith who accounted for a splendid 8lb 6½oz fish in 1978. The North Lake had produced a massive 30lb 3oz mirror to big-fish man Kevin Clifford two years earlier but only a handful of his friends knew it had been caught at Yateley, for Kevin had publicised the fact he had caught this specimen from a Midlands gravel pit! Two anglers who were in the know were Peter Springate and Ken Hodder. These two had been at Yateley on and off since 1975. Ken landed three mirrors from the Match Lake in the summer of 1975 all around the 15lb mark and as the tench men were coming to grips with the North Lake so Pete and Ken tried for the big carp that were now present in this lake. They both saw the 'North Lake fish' (as it came to be known) several times and knew it was a whopper.

Two other prominent specialist anglers, Tim Norman and Terry Lampard, were fishing the North Lake at this time and one morning Tim's indicator flew. Something larger than a big tench had taken his sweetcorn and after a tussle in came a big football-shaped fish. This turned out to be a 20lb common carp. In 1979 it was these four anglers who were pursuing the Yateley carp and very successful they were, for Pete Springate landed the 'North Lake fish' at 31½lb. While Ken Hodder caught two at 14lb and 19lb both from the North Lake, Tim and Terry were concentrating on the other side of the road on a lake which was then named Yateley 2. They fished both the Match Lake and the Copse and at the Match Lake in particular were very successful. They really had these fish going on particles and had many multiple catches of carp to just over 20lb. Both Tim and Terry had caught sight of a big carp in the Copse Lake and Tim managed to hook this fish during the summer only to lose it after a long battle. He was convinced it was a 30-pounder but he never got another chance that year.

1979 turned out to be the year when I ventured forth to find Yateley – it was Len Arbery who tipped me off as to the potential for carp. I had no previous knowledge that Kevin Clifford's fish had come from there. Len told me of other big fish he had seen in another lake known as the Car Park Lake. One July day I drove over to Yateley to see for myself and not knowing what was what I completely missed the entrance to the Match Lake and drove straight into a large car park on the left as you go down Sandhurst Road. Here in front of me was a nice looking lake of some 8–10 acres. I literally followed my nose around this lake, there was water everywhere with just causeway paths in between. As I followed the track I came to the North Lake which was very beautiful and overgrown. Returning back I found myself on the causeway between the North Lake and Car Park Lake, where there were some vantage points in the shape of several trees. Battling through the undergrowth I monkeyed up one of these, the water out in front was shallow and clear and there were the carp, or at least four of them. One mirror, which looked about 25lb, two almost scaleless carp and a much smaller common. They were just basking there. I watched them for some time.

A week or two later I went back to the Car Park Lake and, climbing another tree, I looked down at the water and nearly fell out of the tree! Below me was a fish of such unbelievable size I had to pinch myself to make sure I was not dreaming. It was huge, the largest fish I had ever seen. I thought it must be a record fish and if not it had to be over 40lb. Crazy as it sounds I didn't have my tackle with me. I've often wondered since then what might have happened had I been able to cast to that fish. That afternoon I saw eight different carp. The huge fat one, a mirror which was later named

'Single Scale', two leathers, three commons and just before I left another mirror came in which looked around the 20lb mark. In a daze I walked back to the car determined to return as soon as possible.

As I arrived in the car park a van drew up, the window was wound down and there was the unmistakable beard of Pete Springate and alongside him was Ken. I couldn't contain myself and told Peter and Ken of this tremendous fish I had just seen. Pete asked how big I thought it was, I said: 'I reckon its 40lb'. His next question was: 'What are you doing here, anyway?', with a smile on his face. I knew what he meant. Here was another carp angler who had found Yateley! I managed to catch one of the commons in the Car Park Lake when I returned a couple of days later, it was the largest of the three present and weighed 15½lb. I saw Ken catch one of the others around 12lb on a surface bait as well.

It was only a few weeks later that Ken phoned me late one Sunday night. I was in bed! As soon as he spoke I knew he had caught the big fat one. Of course, he had. 'Go on, guess how big,' I thought quickly, I better not make a fool of myself. I played safe, '38lb–39lb'. Ken said: 'No, it's a 'forty', 42lb, the gut on it is horrible.' Ken had persevered with floaters and tempted the fish the day before. That was the only time that fish was ever put on the bank, in fact we never saw it again from 1980 onwards. That year also saw Peter Springate put one of the leathers on the bank at 26lb, this fish was to become a famous inhabitant in later years. In addition he also landed a very pretty mirror of 20lb 8oz, but quite unintentionally slipped the fish into the North Lake when somebody came down the bank as Ken and he were taking pictures. So that left seven fish in the Car Park Lake. They grew on, and many hours were spent by an ever-increasing band of carp fishermen in the years to come on this particular lake.

With this insight into what had happened in the seventies, let us look, in depth, at the last ten years in the remarkable story of Yateley carp.

The 1980 season dawned with 'carp fever' reaching new heights. Fish of 20lb, regarded as a real milestone even five years before, were now starting to be commonplace, even 30lb carp were coming out almost regularly. In the Surrey/ Middlesex area everyone, it seemed, wanted to catch a carp and the Yateley name was just starting to be put around as a good venue to try. The real pressure, however, would not start for a couple of seasons. I made many close-season visits to familiarise myself with all this water for there were thirteen lakes to look at. It was the Match Lake that drew me most for, on hot days, I spied many good carp basking on the surface in the first bay just over the bridge. On one visit I found a good mirror close to the bank at the North Lake, it wasn't *the* big one but was, nevertheless, another very good one. The Car Park Lake fish were around with 'Single Scale' looking bigger than ever. There was no sign of the 42lb spawn-bound fish that Ken had caught the year before – not really surprising – I am now sure it expired in the 79/80 winter. While on these visits I was surprised that I didn't bump into anyone else who would be looking around, just like me.

As 16 June approached I baited the Match Lake heavily with red kidney beans. One area really took my fancy; there was no swim as such, so I made things a little clearer but not so much as to draw attention to the spot. The season started on the Monday, I intended to start at midnight on the Sunday. That day was Fathers Day and I waited for my mother and father to return from a visit to their caravan at the coast, so I could give him his present (just call me old fashioned). It was seven o'clock before they arrived at the house. I was desperate to get to the lake for I was sure someone else would be there before me right in the swim. I got to the lake at 8pm but there was hardly a soul there. The hard work in the close season paid off, for by 8.30 next morning I had caught a brace of 20-pounders and lost two other carp.

So it continued, I couldn't go wrong. Two other important happenings transpired during that first week. Firstly, I met a chap called Jan Wenczka, a carp angler from Reading who had heard of Yateley carp through Micky Bond. He was to go on and catch many carp from Yateley over the years and has turned out to be my main fishing buddy ever since. Secondly, Terry Lampard, who was fishing for tench in the North Lake, put on the bank the 'North Lake fish' at 39lb taken on 6lb line. Now Terry's only a little bloke and this fish was almost as big as him. It was the same fish which had been first captured by Kevin Clifford back in August 1976, it had been steadily putting on weight since then. It is a very long carp capable of holding a lot of weight. Speculation was rife at the time that here was a carp capable of bettering Dick Walker's record 44lb common. No sooner had I returned home from the first session at Yateley than the telephone went mad with news that a certain Chris Yates had landed a 51½lb mirror at Redmire!

By midsummer another wildly successful Yateley angler hit the headlines – his name Chris Ridington, the fish again the 'North Lake' one, but this time it bettered 40lb for the first time. Chris recorded a weight of 41lb 5oz. In fact Chris Ridington's success at Yateley is hard to match for during the early part of the eighties he caught, in one season alone, forty-seven Match Lake fish including twenty 'twenties'. He landed another famous inhabitant that lived in the Copse called the 'Parrot' at 30lb plus as well as other good ones from some of the other lakes.

By August the 'North Lake fish' was drawing a certain amount of attention from my mate Jan and in spectacular style he hooked the fish one afternoon by fishing from the branches of a tree. The fish pulled him in and he had to swim for it. The most impressive part was the landing for he scooped it onto the bank in his arms! Jan is about the same size as Terry Lampard and pictures of him with that huge carp showed that the fish *was* bigger than him. Its weight had improved to 41lb 10oz. A true monster!

This fish is now, even as we come to the end of the eighties, one of the most sought-after large carp in this country. It is a catchable fish, I don't mean easy to catch but it does, without a doubt, pick up anglers' baits. Of the dozen or so people who have landed the 'North Lake fish', one capture stands out for me, that's when Richie McDonald caught this fish in October 1984. Richie had planned to go to Yateley with Rod Hutchinson during the summer of '84. He knew the fish was growing all the time and here was a chance for him to crack the 40lb barrier. Rod couldn't go in the end so Richie went alone. He first saw the fish when he arrived in mid-August. He put his tackle bag down in the swim he had chosen and he heard an optonic sound. Not taking too much notice, because there were some tench anglers fishing, he didn't realise it was a carp angler who had the run until he heard him shouting: 'I've got the forty on'. Poor Richie thought he had come all this way for nothing, because in truth he was only there to catch that one fish. Sam Fox was the angler concerned and he did land the fish at an incredible weight of 43¼lb. Richie was glad to see the fish. 'It was a beautiful fish,' he later told me. After this Richie returned to the swim he had elected to fish. Sam had told him that the other carp he had seen, when he hooked into the big one, had scattered and gone up to the other end of the lake into the area

Heather, the Leather

Richie recorded the 'North Lake' fish at 45lb 12oz

where Richie intended to fish. As luck would have it he managed to catch an 18lb mirror on that first trip. Although a little disappointed he did not get a look in on the big one, he was pleased to see it and know it was there.

Richie knew comparatively little about the lake at that time but went on natural instincts, watercraft, and where he thought the fish would be. He found that the carp tended to move about a lot and covered a fair amount of water. Bait to catch a fish like this was discussed at length with his mate Rod Hutchinson and it was decided that a high-protein bait, with the flavour Pukka Salmon, would be used. Now into this story enter two young local anglers named Mark Cox and John North for they made a mix, and then baited the North Lake with 9lb of it in the areas Richie had told them, and all they wanted in return was a day's fishing with Rod and Richie. Richie was taking 3lb of bait with him on each visit and making sure it was all going in the water. It took him eight visits (sessions) to put the fish on the bank. Only on the last visit did he have any indication of where the fish might be. It happened that the wind changed to a southerly so he moved on that southerly wind thinking the fish would move also. Then Richie's mate was awoken at 4.30am by an almighty crash, he said it sounded like two cows falling in! He didn't tell Richie until 7am in the morning and directly after he told him he packed up and moved round to where his mate thought he heard the fish and started fishing in that area. With all his concentration focussed on a piece of water between two islands he was rewarded late in the afternoon with a fast run. Instinctively he knew straight away it was the big boy, like most big carp it tended to lumber and wallow rather than race around everywhere. Even so, Richie did well in landing the carp on just a 6lb hook link. But the size of the beast was amazing for Richie recorded the 'North Lake fish' at 45lb 12oz. Truly a 'legend'.

A video was made of the weighing, photographing and returning of the fish. One sequence later showed Richie's delight as he stood by the water with arms in the air and fists clenched, letting out a tremendous victory shout. This event, along with many other notable captures from Yateley in the mid-eighties, made it into a number one attraction. At one stage it seemed there was a mass exodus from other lakes around the country, with literally hundreds of carp men descending on the complex. Some caught fish, many did not, but it didn't matter as they were there, at Yateley, where it was all happening! The attention was mainly focussed on the Match Lake but the other lakes all received a barrage of boilies and particles as well. Of course there were also many of the southern carp men trying hard as well.

One angler who had been at Yateley for a number of years was Robin Dix. Robin had fished most of the lakes for carp and had caught well. But it was his constant determination on the Car Park Lake that reaped the reward of many hours work. In particular, he had watched the growth of one fish over this period and laid a careful plan to bring about its downfall. His baiting campaign was directed in the end to get 'Heather, the Leather' to pick up his hookbait. That over, the next problem was the weed, lots of it. If both these obstacles should be overcome, he knew he had a whopper on his hands. To his credit one day in June 1985 he did just this and when the fish was eventually landed he knew his estimations on her size were correct for here was another massive Yateley carp. In the space of a few short years 'Heather' had put on weight from 26lb in 1981 when Pete Springate had caught her to the weight of 41lb 12oz when Robin landed her. Two separate 40lb plus fish from the same complex put Yateley almost in a class by itself, but there was more to come.

The Car Park Lake also held another whopper which I don't think had been caught up to 1986 but things were about to change for another successful Yateley carp angler was trying very hard at this lake. During the summer he banked this fish and, would you believe, late in the following season this same angler, Keith Sullivan, caught the same fish again. I was present at the weighing this time – the fish weighed in at 35lb. It was, for me, a great thrill to touch this fish and see its immense width and depth for this was the first carp I had seen in the water when I looked into the Car Park Lake all those years before. One day our paths may cross, I wonder?

In the Copse Lake, which is one of the eastern series of lakes, swam another monster. This fish was the one that Tim Norman had first hooked and lost back in 1980. But during the years, this fish, nicknamed the 'Parrot', had been landed by at least four anglers culminating in a young lad putting the 'Parrot' on the bank at just over 39lb. It is one of a number of big fish that are still there in this water. There is a mystery about this lake, it's small, 2½–3 acres, very shallow in the main and, in these last few years, fished very hard by a number of very capable carp fishers but, even with all the modern techniques available, the results are pitifully meagre. Some of these anglers are there because of the stories of even bigger fish, in fact, during the close season of 1985 a local carp angler by the name of Richard Everson who had studied and fished this water in particular spied a real monster. He telephoned me the same evening. He sounded so excited about seeing this fish and ended by saying that it was the biggest fish in the complex. Remember he had been with Richie when the 'forty-five' had been landed. I understand this fish has been nicknamed the 'Pineapple' would you believe! Some anglers think they have also seen this fish although many believe it does not exist so it leaves a nice mystery about the lake.

At least two other lakes within the complex have produced carp in excess of 30lb during the latter part of the eighties as the angling pressure built with visits from so many good carp men from all parts of the country. As we come to the end of the eighties Yateley is now firmly established as a Mecca for carp anglers in the UK. The remarkable 'North Lake' mirror is still one of the largest fish that the serious carp angler in this country can try to outwit. As I write it has proved its superiority again by being caught just a few days before the end of the 88–89 season at a fantastic weight of 44½lb. With fish like that and other big carp on offer, Yateley continues to draw us carp men to its series of beautiful lakes that hold the affection of all those afflicted with the carp 'fever'.

Postscript

With the 1989/90 season only six months old, news comes from Yateley that it has produced its fourth different 40lb plus carp. This fish was caught just before Christmas and weighed 40lb 10oz. Jock White of Ramsgate, a very successful Yateley angler, was the lucky captor.

I have mentioned in the story already that the Match Lake carp never had a chance to attain their maximum weight because of all the fodder fish introduced over the years. Well, here's a fish that escaped – or should I say was moved, quite illegally – into the Weedy Lake on the other side of the road in 1981. Its weight then was 23lb!

8

Wessex Barbel: A Legend in Decline

Pete Reading

Without a shadow of a doubt, the Hampshire Avon has been England's premier big-fish river for many, many years. On its banks many generations of anglers have enjoyed a level of sport that no other river could hope to emulate. Its huge barbel and roach have been celebrated continually throughout the eighties and it is a fact that, during this time, no other river has produced more than a fraction of fish to compare with its number of 12lb plus barbel or 3lb roach. Tragically, however, like most of our chalk-stream rivers, the Avon is in the grip of a serious decline and although local action groups battle to save it, her future is by no means secure.

Pete Reading is a nationally renowned barbel specialist whose catches have been outstanding. Living in Poole puts the Avon and other Wessex rivers right on his doorstep allowing him to get to know the rivers intimately and expertly. Pete has written many magazine articles and contributions to books on fishing the rivers of Wessex. Few, however, are more compelling than this account of the Avon.

The most obvious focal point for the Hampshire Avon's fishermen is Ibsley Bridge. Countless times, in my rovings up and down the Avon Valley, I have been drawn to this spot to reflect after a morning of spotting or fruitless fishing. Stopping at the bridge has almost become a ritual and for many anglers it is an impromptu meeting-place. So often I've got out of my car, strolled up and leaned over the stonework. Looking upstream, to Gorely and Bickton, the salmon pools have names like Botney Pool, Ham Shallows and Hucklesbrook. Downstream, there is the thunderous Ibsley Weir, Hoodies and Cabbage Garden. Names steeped in history and mingling with the coarse fishermen's personal and transient naming of swims – the Aquarian, the Stumps, Dick Walker's Swim, and the Poles. All are scenes of angling triumphs with different meanings to different people.

Just below the bridge is the swim where Charles Cassey landed the Avon's largest authenticated barbel, a leviathan 16lb 1oz, foul-hooked and out of season. I have an old photo of Colonel Crow and Peter Tombleson weighing the fish, unfortunately dead, on Ibsley Bridge. It now gazes down at Ted Waterman's customers in Ringwood Tackle Shop, preserved for all as an example of what the Avon can produce.

Within a fair walk of Ibsley Bridge some terrific barbel and roach have been taken in recent years and often they can be seen from the roadside. With the sun behind me, I've spent many an hour peering into the weed upstream of the bridge and watched barbel drop back under the arches to lie up in safety in the cool dark hole below my feet.

Avon roach in summer are easy to see, yet most difficult to catch. They can often be seen from the bridge delicately weaving their way amongst the ranunculus fronds. Come the winter, they migrate to deeper and steadier water after spending the summer showing off to an enthralled gallery of frustrated anglers.

At 14lb 2oz Pete could hardly believe it!

Although salmon anglers often fish from the bridge it is not a spot I like to fish. The beauty of fishing the Avon is to be found in relative seclusion in delightful surroundings. After a good walk, you can spend a day ensconsed in a quiet reedy swim, watching wild and often previously uncaught barbel or awaiting that firm, bold bite from a roach with a perhaps newly acquired taste for breadflake. Unlike the Stour and despite the ravages of Man's interference, the Avon retains a stately grandeur and intense fishy atmosphere. It winds, weaves, gurgles and rushes smoothly through the flat, lush, green valley, its rich, clear water a home for specimens of most species.

Whether it is because of increased fishing pressure or environmental changes, the barbel and roach are growing and being caught to an increasing average size. When my fishing on the river was at its most intense, an 11lb barbel, or a roach over 2½lb was the target. I remember taking a short fat pig of a barbel of just over 11lb after a three-day stint one autumn. That had me on a wave of euphoria for days. From the same swim came a great roach of 2lb 7oz a few weeks later and I felt I could walk on the surface of the water from Fordingbridge to Christchurch. Targets change with the available fish and bigger fish are available now.

Nowadays, when my corn and hemp supper has been laid out in a gravel run for an evening barbel, I dream of 'twelves', 'thirteens' or more, though often I know they're not in my particular swim. When the quivertip knocks and twiddles, then pulls purposefully round, I hope for a roach over 3lb. Still, any barbel and any roach from the Avon is a special fish and should be valued. I think I've grown out of the biggest is best syndrome and am increasingly content to catch good fish from a lovely river and I hope I shall not stop learning how to do it better and more often. I'm hopeless at trotting for roach and long to hit a big one on the float instead of on the lead.

I want to catch barbel from stretches I've not fished before, or where barbel are only rumoured to lurk. The fewer, the bigger, perhaps! Although baits are perhaps not a crucial factor in success for these river fish, I'd like to try and experiment with some baits that have hardly been used. (Mind you, I think Chris Yates has stolen my idea – the last time we met he was using a daisy, cunningly hooked on as he cast out to tempt some barbel below Ibsley Weir. He pretended it was an accident, a miscast through bankside herbage. I reckon it was hair rigged and daisy is one of the ranunculus family, I think.) Chris has lately forsaken carp, a rather dull fish, for the more exciting barbel, with some success. Frankly, the Avon needs more like him. He blends well with the riverside, his wooden rod merging with the old willow branches, his reel disguised as a piece of discarded farm machinery. Seriously, though, he is a real natural fisherman, with a refreshing attitude. The Avon deserves him.

Thankfully the bulk of Avon regulars are sensible, committed and caring anglers who can appreciate and savour what the river has to offer. Bob Mousley, John Braugh and Gerry Swanton can winkle out 3lb roach in their individual ways, in numbers that make my efforts seem paltry. The river has the richness, variety and potential to respond positively to their individual styles and there are others who are succeeding in tapping this potential without even meeting each other on the bank. There are barbel men at Burgate and Fordingbridge, whose 12-pounders are falling to methods not used at Sopley, Winkton or the Royalty. One man's meat is another man's maggots, yet big fish will fall to both.

The Avon continues to serve as a Mecca to the nation's specialist anglers. In the spring, salmon anglers, including a recently initiated novice like me, ply the holes and deep runs with spinner and Devon minnow in the hope of contacting a fresh-run 20 or 30lb salmon. In early summer, the weed has burst into a green profusion and, on those stretches that allow, barbel anglers wait confidently for the first bold Avon barbel bite, when a gently curved rod leaps into life and a fit bronze 'whiskers' makes its first mistake of the season.

High summer sees the arrival of Avon regulars from all over the country, who settle into quiet reedy swims up and down the river, hoping either for a bag of Avon shoal

The Hampshire Avon (middle reaches)

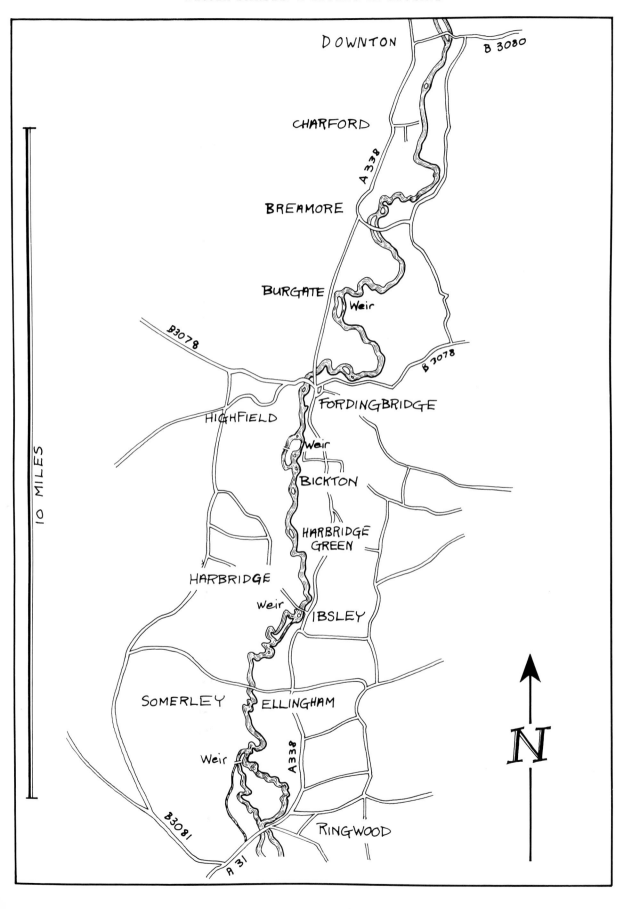

Midsummer on the Hampshire Avon

barbel, spirited battlers in the 4 to 8lb range, or that something special, an Avon double. Most local barbel men wait for the late autumn, when fewer visiting anglers are around, and a slightly coloured, recently flushed river coaxes barbel onto the feed. 'Mists and mellow fruitfulness' – a phrase that sums up the sort of fishing we can experience at this time of year. Great shy barbel that pecked idly at the odd shrimp or caddis may now emerge and have a pre-winter feast, and the river and its surroundings exude a cool, calm, fishy aura – the river's flat glassiness of the summer is replaced by an urgent healthy flow. A time of damp mornings, damp evenings and wet landing-nets in between.

Autumn brings the first of the roach men onto the bank. I caught my first big Avon roach at this time of year, a deep, fat silvery redfin that gulped down maggots meant for barbel. When you are not catching them, they seem impossible, elusive creatures – then a bold bite results in a glorious fish and an apparently easy captive.

The Avon in December, January or February often seems to scream roach – now is the time when a winter evening brings a cold mysterious and seemingly fishless river alive. Gentle swirls start to break the surface and the last hour of daylight sees a host of roach men watching the river, watching their floats or rod tips with intense anticipation. A quivertip that has not moved all day will signal the start of a roachy suppertime with brief plucks and tweaks, then perhaps pull round, provoke a strike and a broad silver shape will thump and flash to the surface. A dogged, awkward fight, and one of those lovely bright Avon roach of 3lb may bring joy to a damp cold angler.

Winter sunset on the Hampshire Avon

Despite its increasing problems, the Hampshire Avon remains a unique, special river, flowing through lovely surroundings. Even if it stops producing huge fish, it will still be worth fishing.

For two days, I had been fishing for quite the biggest barbel I had ever seen. On a little baited patch under my rod tip, it would move in several times a day to grub around, feeding methodically and purposefully in that greedy way that only barbel can. Occasionally, as its great rubbery snout nuzzled the gravel it would turn to one side and display deep bronze flanks and appear to extend to a vastness I'd never seen in a barbel before. After each tantalising feeding spell, it would lift gently in the water, turn casually and cruise off downstream, chomping and working its gills in a satisfied manner. I imagined it resting and burping quietly to itself under a weed-bed while I frantically tried to work out why it wouldn't take my hookbait.

Two smaller fish would often move in while the monster was away and feed with great enthusiasm on her left-overs, sending up streams of bubbles and faint clouds of silt downstream. I determined not to fish for them for fear of scaring off their elder sister and took the opportunity to introduce a little more feed while she was away. The swim comprised a shallow bankside slack, just upstream of a deepish hole, itself surrounded by thick streamer weed. The fish were strange and spooky, scared stiff of terminal tackle and always disturbed when I cast in. I'd seen them before on previous visits, usually as tails poking out behind weed-beds or vague shapes with fins drifting

Pete poses with a fabulous 12lb 10oz Avon barbel

over the dull bottom of the hole. Invariably they had ignored any bait I introduced but now they were at least showing an interest I'd not seen in the two years since I'd found them. I reeled in, checked the hookbait and recast.

A small bomb and a very long tail was needed to avoid scaring the fish. I felt pleased as the bomb settled alongside a small patch of weed upstream of my baited area and the hookbait sank slowly to the bottom. I crept downstream and strained my eyes, searching for signs of the return of the big fish. Two pale blobs were emerging from the darkness of the hole, the huge pectorals of a barbel. The big fish materialised from the gloom and started to feed again. I went back to my rod and focussed on the tip, willing it to move – nothing happened for several minutes – I had gone through this routine before many times. Barbel are always easier to catch when you can see them, sort out where and how they are feeding and place your feed accordingly. Sometimes, however, they persist in teasing and torturing you by pigging themselves over your bait and never going so far as to give you a hittable bite. When really big fish do it, it's even worse.

The Hampshire Avon (including the lower reaches, the Dorset Stour and the Moors River)

84

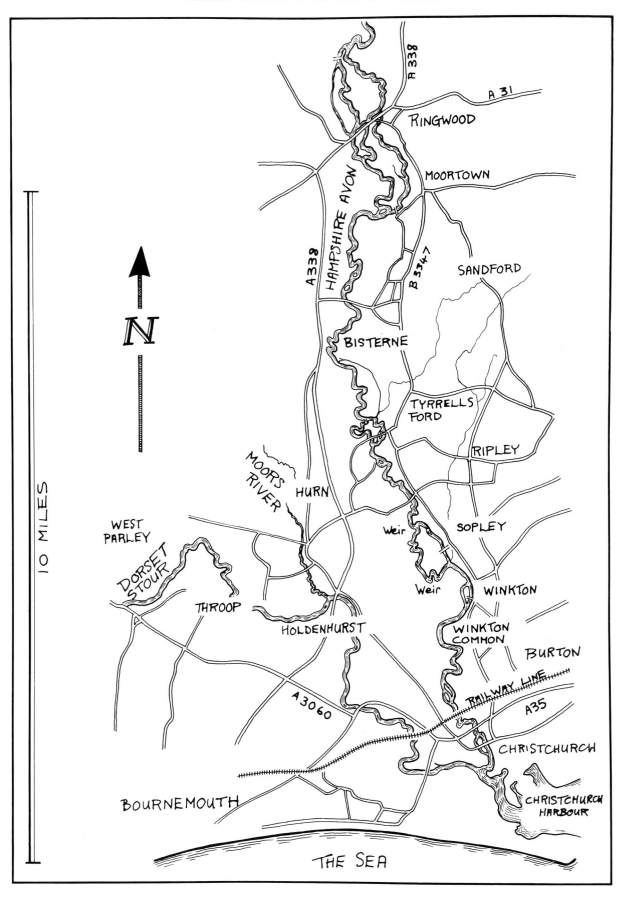

Suddenly the immovable rod curved round in one swift, bold movement. The old Mitchell was backwinding furiously, making that delightful cranky noise that my tired old Mitchells do. I picked up the rod and felt the incredible power and weight of the fish as it shot into the deep water. I saw it turn and flash and thought I'd hooked one of the lesser fish. It looked so small yet as it rose in the water, kicking and shaking its head, it grew and grew and finally thrashed on the surface in a magnificent display of scaly gold, fat white belly and great mahogany fins. Down it went, thumping solidly. There were no scorching runs just deep solid strength under the rod tip. I remember an 11-pounder from Avon Tyrell that had fought in the same way, only to bore down again every time it was pumped to the surface. The old glass rod creaked and strained. I thought about the frayed whippings, the worn rings, the age of the 8lb Maxima, the hook knot, the hookhold. They all held and I blessed the stout round landing-net frame as it pushed aside the thick floating streamer weed and accepted the bulk of a tired and gulping barbel. I could not believe its size. Everything about it was big. The eyes, the barbels, the thick broad pectorals, the paddle of a tail. It was a pigeon-chested, boat-shaped barbel with a girth, depth and length I could not take in. I knew it was a 'thirteen', and when it took the Avons down to 14lb 2oz and a bit, I experienced an elation, a kind of dizzy disbelief I'd never felt before or since. As I gently picked up the fish and felt its weight I was thinking how few other anglers had, or ever would, hold a barbel of such magnitude.

A couple of hours later after further weighing and photographs, I eased the fish from the carp sack and watched it swim off to recover under the dense streamer weed. I wondered if the river would continue to breed and grow such giants and if I would ever come to land such a fish again. Probably not, but I'm still going barbel fishing.

For generations of anglers, the Hampshire Avon has been considered to be the Mecca of coarse fishing. To some extent that statement is still true. Although great bags of dace, roach and chub are no longer a strong possibility, the Avon still offers a quality that is nationally renowned. Quality is the key word here because the small fish population has declined tremendously, to be replaced in part by a head of increasingly larger specimens. In recent years, the barbel, roach and even chub have shown a steady increase in average size and while this trend continues specialist anglers are offered the opportunity to come to grips with fish of near-record proportions.

Ten years ago, a 4lb chub was a rarity on the Hampshire Avon. I remember spending my first three or four years on the river with just one 4lb plus fish to my credit. Nowadays, 4-pounders are becoming as common as they are on the Dorset Stour, where bags of half a dozen or more fish between 4 and 5lb are taken regularly. In the summer of 1988, I weighed a chub of 5lb 7oz for a wild-eyed and grinning Charles Landells who had 'slugged' the fish, a personal best, in his typical manner from under a bush near Ibsley. Five-pounders are now worth trying for and the rumours of 'sixes' could well have some substance.

Roach and barbel are the Avon's most popular specimens these days and although I don't mind chub, it's the redfins and whiskers that draw me to the Avon's banks most regularly. 'A 2lb roach is the fish of a lifetime.' How often in the days of my eager youth had I avidly read every scrap of angling literature I could lay my hands on? Avon fishermen are now fishing for 3lb roach, and there are enough of that size in the river to make catches of two or even three 3lb roach at a sitting a distinct possibility in a few years time.

The Hampshire Avon still holds the official British Record barbel, Joe Day's royalty fish of 13lb 12oz. Never has that record been more precious, because the Avon's barbel are on the increase in terms of individual size. Ten years ago, 12-pounders were almost unheard of, and Andy Orme's 13lb 7oz fish was considered to be a minor miracle when it was reported in the winter of 1983.

Specimens of 12 and 13lb are now reported with very little fuss by the angling press – should the trend continue that royalty fish could fade into insignificance. It is marvellous that we should have the chance to tangle with roach and barbel of these proportions, and the specialist 'specimen' angler, in particular, will say: 'What's all this fuss about a declining Avon?' Sadly, big fish are not immortal, particularly roach, and the current-year classes of big fish may not leave behind enough progeny to maintain the quality of fishing we are enjoying at the moment. Small fish of all species are generally under represented in the river at the moment and unless the problem of consistent fry survival is solved fairly soon, there will be an awful lot of anglers whose Avon fishing will consist of a wistful study of photographs from days of former glory.

The Avon has had to cope with increasing pressures, the least of which is angling. Changes in farming practice have led to the near destruction of the complex water-meadow system, where countless miles of carefully controlled sidestreams and minor carriers offered sanctuary to breeding fish and their fry. Pastoral land has been drained, ploughed and sown with cereals, and subjected to a variety of chemicals to increase yields. Mechanised weedcutting to 'improve' land drainage devastates with ruthless efficiency the underwater weeds, replacing once near-permanent ranunculus beds with a hodgepodge of coarse weed and Canadian pondweed, and disrupting delicate food chains.

Trout farms have proliferated in recent years, and the Avon now has to cope with a burden of effluent comprising of trout excrement and associated chemicals. Rainbow

River Avon Ibsley bridge.
Chris Turnbull 1989

trout escape in their tens of thousands to munch their way through fry as they migrate downstream to the sea. An expanding human population produces an increasing amount of sewage, waste water and road runoff, that tinges a once crystal-clear river with a dull green-grey tint. Golden gravels are now furred with a muddy brown algae, indicating that the Mecca of coarse fishing could soon become but one gravestone in the cemetery of our country's river fishing.

Make the most of it while you can and, even more, try and complain. Write letters, make phone calls, harass the authorities and the officials who make the decisions and control the purse-strings that influence the fate of our rivers. The few who currently make the effort to try and protect our river fishing have finite time, resources and energy. They, and the rivers, need your help more than ever before.

In 1986 Chris Currie, Gerry Swanton and I tried to generate enough enthusiasm in the angling world to petition Parliament about the fate of the Avon. It took us a year of tremendous personal effort, hounding anglers, tackle shops, angling organisations and the press to gather fifteen thousand signatures. This was enough to persuade the Department of the Environment to fund a £100,000 survey of Avon stocks. This work was carried out by the Freshwater Biological Associations River Laboratory team, based at Wareham on the nearby Dorset Frome. This survey highlighted unaccountable gaps in year classes of young fish but with no firm data to compare with, the scientists could come to no firm conclusions. They did, however, strongly recommend further surveys to monitor what the Wessex Water Authority continually and annoyingly calls the 'alleged' decline of the Avon.

Soon we will be calling on your support again. Our newly privatised water authority has the future of our rivers, a national heritage not only held in trust for angling, entrusted to them. We must make sure they do not betray that trust; we must not allow our rivers, and particularly the Avon, to decline any further.

9

Queenford Lagoon: Dream-maker, Heart-breaker

Phil Smith

Since the mid-eighties when Alastair Nicholson, one of angling's great free-thinkers, put Queenford Lagoon in the public eye with his extraordinary pioneering catches of huge bream, the water has become the centre for Britain's big-bream specialists. Through each summer, hardly a month has passed without one of its bronze beauties hitting the angling headlines. Despite this, it remains one of specimen angling's hardest waters ever.

Phil Smith has been fishing Queenford ever since the first of Alastair's catches hit the news and he knows the water as well as any man. He has experienced its highs and persevered stolidly through the many weeks of blanks, in the knowledge that it is merely a matter of time before another Queenford monster is caught and that when it is it may well be a new national record. As one of our most successful all-round specimen anglers, with a tremendous number of big fish to his credit, Phil's specialist approach to big bream has made him the country's top bream angler of today. He has been writing for our angling media for years and has more recently turned his skills to writing books.

Any angler seeing Queenford Lagoon for the first time could be forgiven for thinking that here is just another gravel pit with nothing special to commend it. The water is, however, very special indeed having produced specimen bream to sizes and in numbers that are unprecedented in angling history. At 80 acres, the equivalent of eighty football pitches, it is easy to see what a daunting prospect the water is, providing vast hiding places for the comparatively small head of bream. The water is roughly oblong, the longer banks being situated at the north and south of the pit. The south bank is rather barren of bankside cover, being located only about 20yd from the main Oxford to Reading road, whereas the north bank is more scenic. It is heavily overgrown with bushes and mature trees, most of the swims on that bank having been created by the syndicate members. Once again, a minor road closely skirts this bank. Moving on to the west bank, from where the first bream was taken, we find a mixture of mature bushes, trees and more open rush-fringed areas. The entire east bank is currently out of bounds to anglers as the pit is still being worked by ARC.

The average depth in Queenford is about 10ft, with a maximum depth of 13ft, and there is a relatively small shallow area of 3ft. Everywhere there are numerous gravel bars, some of them very small indeed, and these bars run from 2ft to 7ft above the surrounding bottom contours. Normally, the tops of these bars will be found to be clear of weed while the surrounding deeper water will host solid weed rising very high in the water, often creating extensive surface mats. The bottom composition is obviously mainly of hard gravel but there are deeper areas where deep black mud or very soft silt is found. A further factor is that the weed-beds, which are such an important feature as regards bream location, vary in size and proportion every season. This year's naturally weed-free areas can be next year's dense weed-beds and vice versa.

There do not appear to be any small bream in Queenford, by small I mean fish below about 7lb, and other than the odd tench, perch, pike and chub, the big bream have the water all to themselves. Around the country there must be other similar waters just waiting to be exploited but that is for the future. Queenford is the bream water of today and in the following pages, by relating a few experiences of the last five years, I hope to show the reader just how special a water we have down in Oxfordshire.

Following Alastair Nicholson's capture of a 13lb 14oz bream in 1984, a night syndicate was formed with the full blessing of ARC. The following week, on 25 August, I made my first-ever visit to the water, fishing the north-west corner. I blanked that first trip, a result that was to prove all too common an occurrence. The following weekend, one of the significant events in modern big-fish angling took place. During the week, Alastair had spent some time on the water with an echo sounder, in the company of Joe Taylor, charting the contours and noting the positions of many bars, ridges and other features that abound on a water of this type. During this process, Alastair had noted a gravel bar close to the south bank that he felt warranted particular attention. The stage was set. As the light faded on the first night of my second trip to Queenford, I settled down, again in the north-west corner, while Alastair commenced fishing on that bar.

Phil Smith has every right to look happy with this catch of massive Queenford bream weighing 15lb 14oz, 14lb 7oz and 13lb 12oz

The north bank is more scenic

The day had been hot and sunny and the night was to remain very warm, a light cloud cover holding the temperature at 16°C. I had baited my gravel bar with maggots, hemp and brown crumb and sat in silent expectation. Those people who wonder why we fish cannot know the magic of sitting quietly on a still night, watching the nocturnal wonders of nature slowly unfolding. At around midnight, my eyes were becoming heavy and then Alastair appeared on the bank behind me, casually announcing that he had caught one bream and lost a second. I enquired as to the size of the fish and received the reply that it looked quite big, possibly a new record! Earlier that season, a 15lb 6oz bream, taken from one of the Shropshire meres, had apparently put the record out of reach, and yet here I was about to witness a fish that might beat it. It was a heady moment.

As a member of the NASA Record Fish Committee, I was fully aware of the importance of a correct weighing procedure. Alastair stood by as I carefully set the scales and verified a weight of 15lb 6oz, exactly the same as the Shropshire record. You can imagine the excitement this generated. The second bream from the water had equalled the British record. After congratulating Alastair, I returned to my swim, leaving him to wonder at the possible size of the fish he had lost in the weed.

It was almost a year later when Queenford finally took the record as all the early indications had promised. Friday 19 July 1985 saw me arrive for my normal weekend session. I had decided to fish a bar off the south bank and proceeded to set up my temporary home. Shortly after my arrival, John Knowles arrived and set up midway along the west bank. It turned out later that John had planned to fish a different area but had been forced to change his plans when he found his intended swim already occupied. Fate had dealt him a trump card.

The swim consisted of a 5ft deep bar in otherwise 11ft of water, some 40yd offshore. The bar was fairly narrow front to back and some 4yd across. Placing polystyrene markers at either extremity of the feature, John proceeded to bait fairly heavily, using 15lb of cereal feed mixed with sweetcorn, casters, hemp and wheat. The hookbait was to be two grains of corn and a large lobworm, fished as a cocktail, still one of the most deadly baits today. In the early evening, two baits lay on the top of the bar and John lay back waiting on events.

Throughout the night, numerous line-bites indicated fish activity on the bar but no proper bite materialised. It was daylight, just before 5am, when the indicator at last crept up to the butt ring and a hooked bream plunged for its freedom. John's girlfriend raced round to fetch me, during which time he had sacked the fish and recast. I arrived at his side just in time to see him land his second fish and less than half an hour after the first bite, the third and last bream slid into his net. In thirty hectic minutes bream of 13lb 2oz, 13lb 11oz and 14lb 14oz had been landed. John was obviously elated.

Bream are truly amazing fish, uncatchable for weeks and then apparently suicidal. During the daylight hours, John and I discussed the events of that morning and wondered if the bream would return the following night? Not long after dark, we had our answer as line-bites again started in earnest. However, there was to be a repeat performance of the pattern of the night before. Not once in the dark hours did a bite occur that warranted a strike and it was not until 5.30am that John was again on his feet, playing a truly exceptional specimen. I was soon to be witness to a new record

John Knowles returning his ex-record
15lb 10oz Queenford bream

bream of 15lb 10oz. John was so overwhelmed that he did not even bother to recast his rods and if the bream did have even larger companions, they had a lucky escape. They also missed having their photographs taken for posterity.

Naturally, I was delighted to have been witness to two record bream from Queenford but having spent hundreds of biteless hours on its banks, I was actually hoping to be on the other side of the camera! A couple of weeks after John's tremendous catch, I was to have my chance. On my arrival on the Friday afternoon, I was full of anticipation. There had been no bream activity whatever over the previous ten days or so but conditions appeared perfect. Surely the bream must be due to feed. My first thought was the gravel bar where John had caught, but the two weeks that had elapsed since his catch had seen a mass of dead and decaying weed completely encircle it. I felt that the bream might be reluctant to force their way through it to feed. So I elected to fish a small gravel patch about 80yd out from the north-west corner, possibly 100yd from the scene of John's history-making catch.

After baiting up with brown groundbait, hemp and sweetcorn, I settled back in the gathering dusk. Tackle was fairly standard: 1¼lb test rods, 6lb line armed with size 6 hooks on a short 3in paternoster link. The night was warm and muggy with hardly a breath of wind, the kind of night when expectations really run high. Under these conditions, the odd bleep from the optonic simply had to be caused by fish activity and keeps you alert. After a short time experiencing small indications of this type, at long last the indicator rose smoothly and, after thirty-seven blank nights, I was finally connected to a Queenford bream. Until that moment, the smallest bream to have emerged from the depths of this exciting new water had been John's fish of 13lb 2oz, and so you can imagine the mixed emotions that I underwent when I weighed my first fish of 9lb 12oz. At any other water, a 9lb bream would be an excellent fish but I felt very disappointed after all the effort over two seasons and the countless blank hours. That fish is still one of the smallest ever to come from the water.

As darkness fell on the following night, the disappointment had been replaced by a more positive feeling of suppressed excitement. Using John Knowles' experience as an indicator, it was highly likely that the fish would feed again the second night and I surely could not be so unlucky with the size again. Throughout that night my nerves were on edge, as time after time the optonic would ring out with a single bleep. The strange thing was that only the left-hand rod was affected and I even suspected a fault with the optonic, taking it apart to see whether a small insect had invaded the innards. But I found nothing and when I finally gave up hope of a fish long after daybreak, I was still biteless and totally frustrated. And yet I knew that I had had fish in the area.

During the day I found a possible answer. Straight in front of me was a deep, weed-free area. The weed-beds to the left ended just about level with where the line from the left-hand rod went out to the gravel bar. I reasoned that bream were entering the clear area by swimming over the dense weed and dropping down into the depths as they came to the clearing. Possibly they were clipping the line with their dorsals as they did so. Positioning my boat over the deep clearing, I found it to be around 13ft deep underlain with soft black mud. My normal groundbait would soon sink through this slop and so a different approach was called for. A quick trip to the local supermarket secured ten sliced loaves. The good old standby of mashed bread would be the ideal bait in the circumstances and in the early evening I was again sitting behind my rods, optonics primed, with two baits waiting in ambush in the new area. To assist in the bait presentation, I had lengthened the paternoster links and injected the lobs with sufficient air to make them hover enticingly above the mud and not disappear into it. If the bream did move in, the table was set.

At 11.15pm the first guest came to tea! Agonisingly slowly, the indicator crept up and, following my normal practice, I waited until the line was really tight before I struck. Those anglers who think bream never fight would not have believed the scrap that followed. When I finally netted the fish, I would not have been surprised to have seen a carp or tench in the net. But it was a bream all right, a fish that finally rewarded me for all the long fruitless nights. I was on cloud nine as I verified 14lb 15oz. As has happened so often with Queenford fish that first bream was quickly followed by another which fought just as hard. At one stage during the scrap, everything went solid, and I am convinced that the fish dived so hard into the bottom debris that it actually partially buried itself in the ooze. Only with a liberal application of brute force was it extricated and found to weigh 12lb 12oz; the last bite that season.

During the early weeks of the 1986 season, several bream came out quite quickly and Andy Flanders, in particular, achieved great success having four good fish in a short space of time. His best was exactly 14lb. On the Friday night which heralded the start of my fortnight summer holiday, I arrived at Queenford to find the syndicate very well represented. That season, most of the fish had been taken off the north bank and all the known swims there were already taken. What had been unusual over the previous week was that indications from bream had been apparent in more than one swim at a time, which hitherto had been unknown.

Surely the bream must be due to feed

94

Baiting the swim for another hopeful night

Tony Miles was in one swim where line-bites had been occurring over the previous two nights, without any positive indications to strike at, and it was obvious that bream were passing to and fro along a fair stretch of bank, without getting their heads down. It had to be a matter of time. Chatting to Tony, it transpired that he had to leave the next day and he suggested that my best option would be not to cut a new swim but move into his swim after he had vacated it. I had the choice also of fishing the west or south banks in the hope of contacting fish from a different shoal but it was a long shot. I decided therefore to sit with Tony that night and set up my gear in the swim the following morning.

All night long we talked and drank endless cups of tea while the line-bites returned as soon as darkness fell. For at least two hours the bobbins jumped up and down continuously with Tony on the edge of his seat. It was a nerve-wracking night and an hour before dawn there came the one positive bite. It had all the indications of a true bite but although Tony did everything right, he struck into nothing. Moments like these are heart breaking at Queenford after weeks or months of effort. After breakfast Tony packed his gear and set off for home with his message of good luck ringing in my ears.

With the whole of the day to set up my tackle and my camp, I could take things very casually. It never ceases to amaze me the quantity of gear we take to the bank for an extended stay. I've always said that if reincarnation is true, then I'll come back as a donkey! The swim was a gravel bar only about 40yd out from the bank, completely devoid of weed on its top, but surrounded by very dense weed in the deep water alongside the bar. Before baiting, I also went out on my boat and, with my long handled rake, scraped the top of the gravel to remove any vestiges of weed that were present and stir up any insect life that could encourage the bream to investigate.

As dusk descended, the wind changed direction and picked up force, blowing directly into the swim. Queenford's alternative name is Cootsville, because of literally hundreds of these water birds that spend their entire waking lives ripping up weeds, which then rise and float along the surface at the mercy of the wind. This drifting flotsam can be a nightmare at times. That night I had one positive indication which, like Tony's the previous night, was missed. The rest of the night was spent clearing weed from the swim and off the lines. Dawn came and still no bites, and by about 9am the chance had gone.

The very slow nature of the Queenford fishing means that the members of the night syndicate are all serious and dedicated big-fish anglers. It does not, however, prevent us from having a little fun and relaxation in the day when there is nothing else doing. A few games of chess, Scrabble tournaments and endless cups of tea while away the hours and soon it is time to start preparing again for the night ahead.

That second night was mild and calm, the annoying wind of the previous evening having died. About half an hour after dark, the indicators started to betray the presence of fish. There was nothing decisive but enough to keep me on my toes. Finally, at about 2.30am, one indicator slowly lifted to the rod. I waited for the line to tighten and then struck, feeling a satisfying thump as I connected. There were two more heavy plunges and then nothing. The fish was off! My feelings at that moment are hard to describe. Queenford chances are too rare to miss, you could literally wait months or years for the next one. Keeping my annoyance under control, I rebaited with three grains of corn and lobworm cocktail and recast. Would that lost fish have scared any others off the bar, or was he the only bream in residence? At 3am I was answered as the indicator rose again and this time the hook held. In the bright moonlight, I could see the bream as it kited across the surface towards the trees to my left and before long it was safely in the net. The other syndicate members joined me in the weighing ceremony and confirmed a weight of 13lb 7oz. After I had recast for a second time, I could relax. I had another Queenford prize in a sack for the morning photo roll-call.

There was another act to the drama well after daybreak. Yet again, the indicator rose smoothly and I was playing a big bream. As this was my first bream in daylight, I could see that it really was big. There were several heart-stopping moments as it fought on the surface but eventually Andy Flanders netted it for me. Before long, we had established that the bream was my personal best, with a weight of 15lb 3oz, and a length and girth of 26½in and 25in respectively. Truly a dustbin lid!

It was Monday evening, 4 July 1988, when Derek Quirk rang to enquire what was happening at Queenford and I relayed the events of the season so far. Bream had been caught in the first couple of weeks but things had gone very quiet again. What had been noticed, however, was that the swims along the west bank were now almost totally devoid of weed, whereas the previous season they had been virtually unfishable. Conversely, the north bank, which had been clear the previous season, was now solid! I had already decided to fish 'Knowles' Bar' the following weekend and Derek kindly agreed to leave that swim alone when he arrived in midweek.

When I arrived on the Friday, Derek was just moving to a swim we know as the Mud Flats, about 100yd down the bank from Knowles' Bar. On the previous two nights, he had fished the bar on the south bank that had produced the 15lb 6oz fish to Alastair Nicholson four years before but to no avail. I found Mark Chivers encamped in the swim I had intended fishing, so I set out my stall in an adjacent swim, from where there was another good feature to fish at. It was the swim from where the very first Queenford fish had been taken.

It had not been dark very long when there were signs of fish activity all along the bank. In front of me a large bream back broke the surface and we all sat in excited suspense. Just after midnight an optonic sounded and Derek Quirk went into action. He was fishing a long way out so, without hesitation, he made his way to the water's edge, between the trees that bordered the cramped little swim, and clambered into the waiting boat. This was another bream that had not heard the rumour that bream do not fight because Derek was convinced that he had hooked one of the carp that the water was supposed to contain. After a very memorable fight, a big bream finally slipped into the landing-net. It was an unbelievable fish of 15lb 8oz. If he never had another bite, the success of Derek's season was assured. Even so, he rebaited the hook with a special cocktail of corn, casters and a large lob. How could any self-respecting specimen bream resist that?

An hour later, once more Derek found himself rowing into the blackness to net another giant fish, this time of 15lb 9oz. After only one hour, he had a new personal best! With two big bream in the sacks, the indications still continued unabated and by 6am he had added another three bream to his tally, fish of 14lb 6oz, 14lb 6oz and 12lb 5oz. Just how do you follow a catch like that? Derek was elated while Mark and I were just pleased to have been part of an historic occasion. We had actually stopped fishing ourselves to stand and watch Derek as the events of the night had unfolded.

Convinced that he had made the catch of a lifetime, Derek generously invited Mark and me to fish the swim the next night. Previous experiences suggested that the bream had a good chance of feeding there again. As darkness fell, Mark and I were rapt in intense concentration, willing the indicators to move while Derek, very understandably, had taken a break and was celebrating his catch in a local tavern. When he eventually returned to the lake, he fished for a while and then retired to his sleeping bag.

Dawn came and went and still Mark and I were biteless. Derek was now awake and strolled along the bank for a chat. As we stood talking, we distinctly saw a bream break surface on the bar in front of Derek, the same bar that Mark and I had fished the previous night. Derek wasted no time in baiting his hooks and casting out. He did not have long to wait, the first bite coming very quickly. This time, the fish fought poorly but its sheer size made up for that. At 15lb 12oz it was a veritable goliath of a bream. He had beaten his best yet again. Once again, his bobbins were bouncing up and down and we all awaited the inevitable. Sure enough, another bite was not long in coming, this time resulting in his last fish of 15lb exactly. Mark and I worked out that if we had not changed swims, I would have caught the 15lb 12oz fish and Mark the 15-pounder. How could we possibly be jealous of Derek though. He had unselfishly invited us to share in the fun in a swim in which we all expected further bream to feed and had been justly rewarded for his generosity.

The catch of fish to Derek Quirk has set an imposing target for the rest of the syndicate members, who will now be trying to better it or to catch another British record, a fish that undoubtedly swims in Queenford. We are all sure that a 17lb fish will emerge eventually. As for Derek, he went on to fish a further thirty nights without so much as a twitch. That is the challenge of bream fishing at Queenford Lagoon.

10
Wensum Barbel
Steve Harper

Steve Harper is a native of Norwich in Norfolk. Unlike most of the other contributors to this volume, he seldom ventures far from his home territories for his fishing. Despite this, he has made a very significant name for himself in the big-fish scene. One of Steve's earliest major triumphs was the capture of an 11lb 14oz specimen barbel, a new record for the River Wensum. Barbel had been introduced into the Wensum some while before this but had managed to avoid capture; however, now that Steve and a few friends were pioneering their capture, all that was about to change.

Before long, the Wensum was acclaimed as one of the country's finest big-barbel fisheries and throughout the eighties few summers passed without its big fish appearing in the angling press. Throughout that period Steve remained one of the most consistent anglers on the river.

Steve, at one time, made fairly regular contributions to angling magazines, but more recently has turned his attention to writing books.

Much of its course flows through some of Norfolk's most beautiful and unspoilt countryside

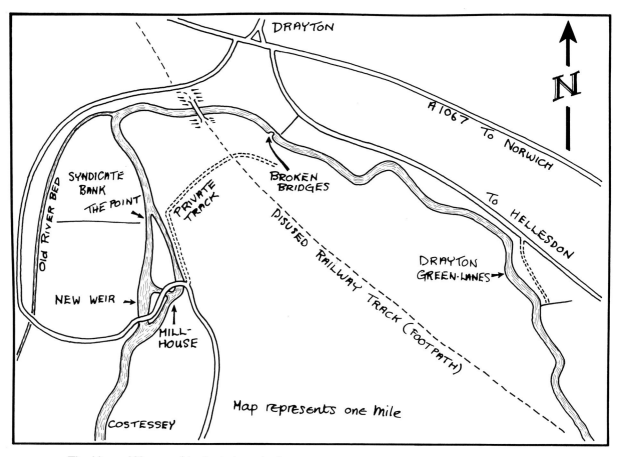

The Upper Wensum (the barbel reaches)

Saturday 19 February 1972. It was the first time that John Judge and I had fished 'The Marshes' stretch of the River Wensum for chub that winter. After the long walk along the railway track, turning left across the fields, we made a late start at around 10.30am but the weather was forgiving. Overcast and cold, but without rain, we knew the chub would feed.

After baiting several swims with cheese paste, John had the first action. Two chub coming in quick succession, soon followed by another, this time to my rod. From then on, it was all go. Bites were confident, coming fast and furiously throughout the morning and into the afternoon. Some were missed but by 3pm we had amassed a total of fourteen chub including several 4-pounders, the largest scaling 4lb 9oz, a personal best for me at that time.

Following a pricked fish, my swim had died and I introduced more bait before finally inducing another pull to the quivertip. A much more vicious bite than any previously encountered, it almost took the rod from its rest as the fish headed abruptly downstream, taking my rod tip with it. The slipping clutch unaccountably did not slip and before I realised what was happening, the fish had pointed the rod, finally snapping the 5lb breaking strain line with a sharp crack as if it were cotton. I was shocked and bewildered. I could not understand the power of the lost fish. How could any chub be so much more powerful than another, regardless of size? The tackle had handled many chub, some large, so easily until this final monster had been hooked.

I considered other species, but at that time I knew of no other in the Wensum that could be responsible and in my naivety I put the culprit down as a chub of at least 6lb.

It was many years later I learned that even as early as 1959, barbel had been stocked into the River Wensum albeit in very small numbers. I did eventually put two and two together, realising that on that bleak, February day way back in 1972, I had had my first encounter with the barbel of the River Wensum.

The Wensum is an exceptional river in many ways. Only in size does it lack stature. Even at its widest points, in the City of Norwich, just before it is joined by the much smaller River Yare to become, unjustly, the River Yare, it is no wider than a few rod lengths. But what it lacks in size it amply makes up in beauty, atmosphere and charisma. Classed as one of the very few remaining Class 'A' river fisheries left in Norfolk, the picturesque barbel stretches between the mills at Costessey and Hellesdon are narrow and often shallow. Whatever species inhabit the Wensum here they usually grow to considerable size. Much of its course flows through some of Norfolk's most beautiful and unspoilt countryside: woodland, fields and marshland, much of it secluded and private, and populated by kingfisher, fox and water vole.

In summer, weed growth is prolific along most stretches, choking the river from

Steve Harper with a 10lb 3oz barbel, one of his many Wensum doubles

John Wilson with 'Bo', one of the Wensum's most well loved fish, this time weighing 12lb 12oz

bank to bank, river bed to surface until the water authority, in its wisdom, sends out the dreaded weed-cutting boats. It is unfortunate that the areas deemed most in need of cutting are also the main areas most favoured by the barbel for spawning. In the past, action through the Anglers Consultative has helped this problem to some degree. In early summer the crystal-clear shallows abound with fry of many species and sizes. For a variety of reasons, including abstraction by the new Norwich water supply pipeline directly above the barbel reaches, and agricultural pollution and runoff, most of these small fish do not survive to maturity. Having said that, the barbel do share the river with a multitude of species including chub, dace, eel, roach, tench, carp, bream, perch, pike, grayling, gudgeon, minnow and even crayfish in a few remaining areas, and it is not uncommon to latch into the occasional surprise when fishing along the Wensum. But it should be noted that the majority of fish stocks are often very localised and, sometimes, large stretches are totally barren of any notable fish at all.

In the past the Wensum was justly famous for its deep-bodied, blue-backed and gigantic river roach. But as with everything in angling, nothing is forever and the

I was playing a very large and anxious barbel

shoals of Wensum two-pounders are now sadly only a memory in the diaries of a few Norfolk anglers. There are still roach in the Wensum, some very large, but compared with the mid-seventies, when the vast roach shoals reached a peak, their numbers are almost insignificant and it is the barbel that has now become synonymous with the River Wensum. I wonder how long they will reign?

During their brief history, these barbel have become something of a legend in angling circles. Rarely does a month pass by in summer and autumn without a large barbel from the famous River Wensum gracing the pages of the weekly angling publications, giving its captor a taste of fleeting fame if not fortune. It was during the summer of 1972 that the main stocking of the Wensum at Costessey took place (although small numbers had been introduced some years prior to this in 1959 and 1967). In August of that year, the Severn River Authority released 247 barbel up to 7lb in weight to two other river authorities. Seventy-nine barbel went to the Sussex River Authority for their rivers Adur, Rother and Ouse and 168 barbel to the East Suffolk and Norfolk River Authority.

These fish had been electrofished from the River Severn at Atcham during a three-day operation following a survey conducted by Dr Peter Hunt of Liverpool University. This survey found the Severn barbel thriving to such an extent that the river was in danger of becoming overstocked with stunted barbel. It is interesting to note that these Severn fish were in turn descendants of a similar operation in 1956, organised by *Angling Times*, when 509 barbel had been transferred from the Kennet to the Severn. Of the 168 barbel released to the East Suffolk and Norfolk River Authority, there was rumour that a small number had been released into the River Yare. But undoubtedly the majority were put into the Wensum at Costessey and very soon became established in their new home.

Mr Ellis, then clerk to the river authority, asked anglers in the area to respect the new arrivals and give them a chance to become accustomed to their new surroundings. He also asked that they be treated with great care when caught and, in particular, he advised that they were not to be retained in keepnets due to the known problem of the serrated edge of the dorsal fin tangling with the mesh. For the first five years they were left pretty much alone and little was heard of them. Only rarely was a barbel caught and then usually by accident and of no great size. It seemed the Wensum was an ideal river, catering for all the demands of our largest non-predatory river fish and they adapted well but were not often seen. No one realised how well some of these fish had adapted, growing from the maximum stocking size of 7lb to an incredible 12lb in five years. Chub remained the main quarry for the Norfolk river angler looking for large fish (a much more prolific and obliging species). And so it was for me until one day in the long hot summer of 1977 when river fishing took on another dimension.

July 1977 was drawing to a close. The summer so far had been hot, almost as hot as the previous year but now had deteriorated into overcast skies and constant drizzle. Whilst chub fishing, Mike Saunt and I had stumbled upon a shoal of barbel, located beneath the branches of an alder tree, overhanging a fast, gravel run flanked by streamer weed. It was the first time we had encountered barbel in any numbers and having never caught a Wensum barbel, we were very excited about our discovery.

We spent our first session experimenting with different baits to see what they would accept or even recognise as food. Mike had hooked a small barbel from within the branches of the alder only to lose the fish almost immediately, but by the following day, the shoal had re-formed and I decided to try again. They seemed to favour this swim very strongly and, on my return, I found two small barbel in residence and several medium-sized chub, followed shortly by a much larger barbel. After some further bait experimentation and two abortive casts, I finally managed to present a bait to the largest fish from almost directly above, perched precariously in the branches of the alder, my large carp net placed strategically at its base.

After perhaps an hour – it seemed much longer – the big fish accepted my bait and before I realised what was happening I was playing a very large and very anxious barbel from within the branches of the tree. The hardest task was to descend the tree, whilst still keeping in contact with the fish, and reach the net below. Somehow I managed and after wading out in Wellingtons, I netted my prize with difficulty and returned to the bank with squelching feet. I had estimated this fish, the largest in the swim, at 8 to 9lb. With no experience of barbel, I had little on which to base my judgement and was shocked when the needle kept spinning around the dial on the Avons. It was the great girth and depth of the fish that I had not accounted for and after the weight of the landing-net had been subtracted, a weight of 11lb 14oz was recorded. Norfolk's first double-figure barbel.

The fish shocked the local angling community but it was no fluke fish, contrary to some areas of local opinion at that time. It was followed two months later by a little publicised 10-pounder caught by a holidaying angler, F. Gibbs from Essex. I had also observed several other fish that I was sure approached double figures and realised that there were perhaps many barbel in the Wensum of a similar size. In the next two

Norfolk's first double figure barbel

Chris Turnbull 89.

seasons I was also fortunate to land double-figure barbel and by then, other anglers had taken an interest.

The Wensum barbel continued to grow and in 1980 Arthur Clarke of Norwich captured a beautiful specimen of 12lb 4oz, a new river record. Three years later this, in turn, was surpassed by a fish of 12lb 12oz, captured by Trefor West of Coventry, an angler who was to become one of the most consistent captors of Wensum barbel. Less than a year passed and Dave Plummer landed one of the largest known fish in winter when it weighed a massive 13lb 6oz. This particular fish is known to freewheel throughout the year between a little over 11lb and 13½lb. Measuring 31in in length, it is easily distinguishable by a distinctive deformed tail fin, a long spur along the top edge and the absence of a 'V'. I captured this particular fish in the summers of 1986 and 1987 when it weighed 11lb 6oz on both occasions.

The barbel can be observed spawning during most years and this can be a truly amazing sight as many fish, some in excess of 12lb, throw caution to the wind and enter the gravelly, shallow runs to act out their annual spawning ritual. However, few fry seem to make it through to become adult fish. Small barbel of less than a 1lb have

Left: The big fish materialised from the gloom

been caught but very rarely. In 1987, a fish of 1lb 14oz was taken by Trefor West. The smallest I have caught weighed 4lb 12oz and it seems the population can just about hold its own against mortalities. This, in one way, is an advantage to the angler in that a high average weight is maintained but the low number limits the areas that can be inhabited by barbel.

Since the mid-eighties, due to angling pressure, the barbel has become progressively harder to catch in any numbers, becoming accustomed to the more conventional baits and methods employed by many anglers. Hair rigs are in common use although I personally do not use them for barbel apart from when using hemp as a hookbait. Corn and meat are now shied away from although occasionally a fish, often a large one, will still pick up one of these baits, making some angler's season a memorable one. But to catch consistently, a little more thought and originality is required. Maggots mixed with hemp, lobworms (always a first-class barbel bait), if you don't mind a few eels, and paste baits now all account for big barbel. Boilies I have not used, not because I think they wouldn't catch, indeed I know of some barbel that have succumbed, but because I prefer to catch my barbel on more traditional baits. As for bite indication, I am less traditional, shunning the rod or quivertip in preference to a monkey climber and a rod if possible, pointing straight at the bait. With this set-up, the rod-wrenching barbel bite is less common, the rod tip an automatic bolt rig. The monkey climber allows a length of slack line and the bites can be seen to develop, some uncharacteristically slowly for barbel!

The barbel population at the moment seems stable, although the really large fish of 11lb plus do seem fewer than several seasons ago – 7-, 8- and even 9-pounders are not uncommon but fish of less than 5lb are rare. In recent seasons, I have identified at least seven different doubles in the known barbel stretches but if the Wensum does hold any surprises in the shape of unknown gigantic barbel, it will be from areas other than the usual barbel haunts. Angling pressure, I believe, is also having an adverse effect on some of the larger Wensum barbel. The two largest known fish in recent seasons have begun to weigh less. Whereas in the mid-eighties it was not uncommon for them to reach and even exceed 12lb, they now weigh only ounces over 11lb and it is possible that the Wensum has already peaked, unless some of the 9- and 10-pounders continue to grow and finally challenge the largest of the Wensum's barbel. This could possibly be happening already as I did have an interesting session in an area not known as a barbel haunt in the summer of 1988.

I had been searching out new barbel lies and on the last day of July was finally successful. It was mid-morning, hot and close but overcast. The swim was an unusual one in which to find barbel. It was a small shallow cattle-drink bordered by a thick band of weed where the crystal-clear water dropped steeply away and became faster. From high within the overhanging tangle of alder and stunted oak, I could observe every detail of the swim down to the pebbles on the river bed and it was not difficult to spot the head of a large barbel just protruding from the dense border of weed, almost perfectly still. Chub milled all around, as voracious and food-searching as ever but the barbel seemed unimpressed.

I dropped in a few hookbaits to trundle down towards him but he remained unmoved, even as the chub stole his intended snack. Other tactics were called for. With difficulty, I managed to set up a rod from within the branches and lowered a dropper full of hemp into the flow just above the swim. Gently, it sank, hitting the bottom and releasing its scented cargo in a cloud of seeds that soon settled in the dips and crevices of the gravel. Hemp is an enigma – almost the magic bait – no other has such an hypnotic effect upon fish. It *is* a drug to some fish, especially barbel, and they find it impossible to resist. This is, of course, common knowledge and I had previously caught many barbel as a result of baiting with hemp but to see its startling powers at first hand and at such close quarters was staggering. Almost before the dropper had completely emptied, the previously disinterested barbel was out of its lie and mopping up the seeds, discolouring the water in a frenzy. I estimated it to be about 9lb and strangely light coloured. But more surprises were in store!

Seconds passed and another barbel, larger than the first, just seemed to materialise beside the other, also searching out each and every tiny grain. This second fish did seem more cautious, coming into the swim and out again repeatedly, pausing only to take a few mouthfuls and then retreating to the deeper, weeded edge. I risked another dropper of hemp into the swim. From above I did not need to cast and could simply lower the dropper into the river, thereby avoiding the fish-scaring splash. The extra hemp juices worked immediately and the larger fish returned, this time feeding without caution and, incredibly, bringing with it yet another barbel of even larger proportions! The three fish fed avidly for quite some time but seemed oblivious to my hookbaits. Eventually, as the clouds thickened and a steady drizzle began to fall, they left the swim but I was sure that towards evening, they would return and feed harder and longer as dusk fell.

It was interesting to reflect on the morning. If I had not introduced the hemp, I would simply have seen one stationary barbel disinterested in feeding. As it was, the hemp had moved the barbel into feeding and pulled into the swim two very large, unseen barbel that must have been very close by, or hidden in the dense weed beneath me. I could not recognise these two larger fish but they were both easily into double figures, the last very long, possibly a 12-pounder if it had the girth and depth below.

That evening I returned and was dismayed to find the swim occupied on the far bank by an angler and his two sons plus dog. I just could not fish anywhere else. My heart was set on this swim alone and so I returned home, hoping that the three barbel would favour the cattle-drink swim the following evening. And so they did! I watched and baited them for quite a considerable time from the trees with droppers of hemp and hookbait samples.

The evening was overcast, still and misty and as the light began to dim around 8pm, I lowered my first cast over the screen of reeds and into the swim. Line-bites plucked at the monkey climber almost immediately and after only twenty minutes it hurtled towards the rod, the rod tip arching over and I was on my feet, battling with, I was sure, one of the three. I held the fish hard to prevent it covering the short distance to the fringe of deep water where the thick weed began. But to no avail. Within seconds the barbel had ploughed into the weed and I had to walk downstream changing the angle of pressure and gradually moving the fish from its sanctuary. There was no letting the fish return and I netted it with the weed at the first attempt and eagerly separated the two to see which of the three barbel I had captured. The light colouring of the fish soon told me it was the smallest of the trio, the first one I had seen in the swim and it weighed 9lb 5oz.

I rested the swim, rebaited it and finally fished through until almost midnight but without further sign of action. Those two mysterious barbel had left the swim and over the following evenings, did not return, lost somewhere amongst the depths and weed-beds of a truly outstanding barbel river – the River Wensum.

11
Fenland Zander: After the Goldrush
Neville Fickling

The predatory zander, perhaps the most controversial of our alien species, was introduced into Norfolk's Fenland drains as a water authority experiment. It was later blamed for the eventual decline of the Fens as fisheries by the same authority, who in response, waged a massive cull against the species. Many anglers, however, are of the opinion that the zander was in fact made into a scapegoat and that the actual cause of the decline was due to intensive farming practices and, more importantly, poor water management by Anglian Water itself.

As a consequence of this debate, angling came out in two camps in a love-hate relationship with the species. In one camp the matchmen and others who have an inbuilt bias against all predatory fish which live on the small fish they so like to catch. In the other camp, the specimen anglers who mourned this attempt at the eradication of the species. After all, whatever the truth behind the decline of the Fens, the zander had provided them with some fantastic sport over the years.

By the later half of the eighties zander were still comparatively few and far between on the Fens; however, what they lacked in numbers they made up for in weight. Neville Fickling, as a native of the Fens, grew up with the species and is probably the most successful angler ever to specialise in post-cull zander fishing.

First encounters are often well remembered though later events may take some deep thought to recollect. That first encounter was in November or December of 1966 at Magdalen Bridge on the Great Ouse Relief Channel. This is where the zander's spread throughout the country really started. My crucian carp live-bait fished under a homemade sliding float was taken again and again, but each time I wound down there was nothing there. The bait came back slashed to ribbons. For the life of me I couldn't understand it, I don't think I even knew that zander existed at the time. Yet, a year later I had seen my first zander, a small one from Downham Market bridge. Another year passed before I had caught one. Two of us caught seven fish from the mouth of the Polver drain on the Relief Channel up to 3lb 4oz. It was a hectic evening session with many missed runs. I can just about remember the marvellous feeling of elation we had then, trying for zander for the first time and doing so well. Typically those results were not to be repeated in the immediate future but that is zander fishing for you.

Since those days I have fished for zander every season on a large number of waters. I've even fished in Holland although I've yet to catch one there! On looking back at Fenland zander fishing I think that the whole twenty years can be broken down into four sections, not necessarily related chronologically, but more to do with water and weather conditions and the times of capture of the majority of zander. These four phases serve to show how varied the behaviour of the zander can be, even in the same waters. It will show how interesting they are to fish for. The four phases are:

1   Floodwater, winter, autumn and summer.

Dawn on the River Delph sees the last chance of a fish fade away

2 Usual behaviour so typical in the early seventies when dusk and dawn were the times to catch zander.
3 The late seventies when bright sunny days seemed to be the key to zander fishing.
4 The nocturnal phase, which seemed to start in the mid-eighties and is with us now.

My first introduction to floodwater zander was in the summer of 1968; the fact that there is a Pink Floyd song called 'Summer 68' is only of incidental interest at this stage! The summer of 1968 was very wet and for much of the time the Relief Channel was running off and very coloured. I did not know then that zander are quite at home feeding in such conditions. To me one day was very much like another. I just went fishing! Having already caught a few zander, the news of a 9lb and 8lb fish from the channel at Stowbridge was enough to get me on the train to Magdalen Road Station and then cycle the extra 3 miles to Stow. I had seen a 9lb zander in my local tackle shop and I dearly wanted to catch one like it. Little did I know that both the 8- and 9-pounder were the original stock fish, two of the ninety-seven released into the fishery.

I think much of the attraction of zander fishing was that it was technically quite easy. After all, there is nothing easier than legering a small, dead fish. Little boys have been doing this in the Fens for years and they still catch zander today. I suppose that if any degree of sophistication had been required we would have rapidly lost

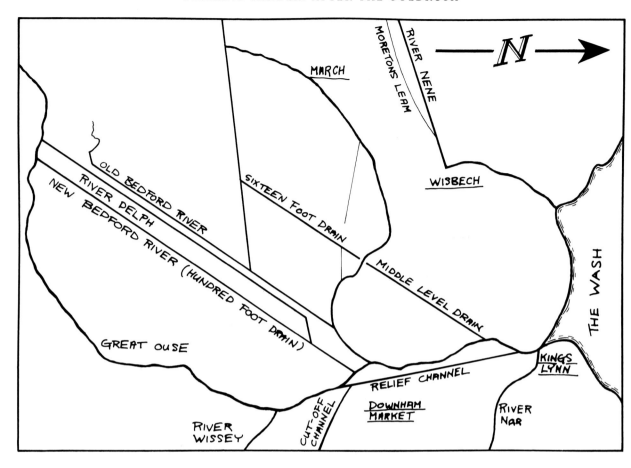

The Fens

interest. Our tackle was basic, typical of fifteen year olds but I, at least, had a 9ft glass rod and a 10ft Chapman 500 cane rod, so I could fish two rods. I cannot remember what we used for bite indication, I think it might have been a slack clutch with a spinner hung on the line between reel and butt ring. Whatever it was we caught zander. The small dead roach was hooked through the tail with a size 1/0 single hook and the only trace we used was 20lb line. A ½ or ¾oz bomb seemed enough to cast the baits out into the water where the zander were hunting in the muddy water.

It is funny to think that by pure accident we were fishing in a manner ideally suited to zander. We did not know that zander take most of their prey tail first, yet we just happened to have the hook in the tail! That first trip to Stow produced a 7-pounder to my rod, another original stock fish. We did not know this at the time, but it should have been clear to anyone who knew much about the original introduction. There had to be a big gap in zander sizes simply because there was three years difference between the original stock fish and their progeny. During those floodwater conditions zander were caught throughout the day, a trend that was to be repeated during autumn and winter when the rivers were in flood. The zander were stimulated by the floodwater and because of their superior vision they proceeded to hunt for prey around the clock.

A few years later with more normal water conditions, zander began to be caught with predictable regularity at dawn and dusk. The water was clear and this may have been the reason for frantic feeding spells as the light intensity changed. So often three or four runs would occur just as dawn broke or all rods away at once as the sun set. Night fishing was almost a waste of time and believe me we did a lot of that! As the season went on and winter approached, cooler weather brought even shorter feeding periods. These were the days of one zander run at dawn and then nothing, save hopefully for the odd pike! Finally any cold weather at all would leave you thinking there were no zander in the water.

Then just as we had got everything figured out, the zander on many waters opted for feeding in the middle of the morning or in the afternoon. If it wasn't bright and sunny they didn't feed. If this had just happened on the Delph or the Middle Level we would have put it down to different venues responding differently, however the Relief Channel zander must have been feeding in sympathy with the others because they followed exactly the same pattern. It was good fun in those days, arriving just before the witching hour, catching a few zander as predicted and then moving elsewhere!

Then in the eighties the zander, just about everywhere, decided night-time was the right time. Everyone had to get out their bedchairs and sleeping bags. The story that follows recounts the three seasons when I spent many of my summer and autumn nights alone on the banks of various fen drains. The fishing was good and at one stage I actually hoped I did not get too many runs, because I needed the sleep! I've since regretted getting so laid back in my zander fishing. A year's struggling gets you back to reality!

Over the years I have fished most of the Fenland drains and stillwaters for zander. The summer of 1986 saw me return once again to the River Delph, mainly because my other venues had proved far too difficult in the past two seasons. The odd few trips in June and July were not notable for the number of big zander, though the 21lb 3oz carp taken on a legered live-bait did liven things up a bit! However, by August things were

Neville with a magnificent 13lb zander caught in 1989

beginning to pick up with several good zander to 8lb 5oz taken. The interesting thing was that daylight activity was almost nil, with all the runs coming at night. Even an idiot 18lb pike decided for several nights to get in on the action! Legered dead-baits, mainly small roach, were working well and problems with small eels were mercifully few.

Luck was almost to desert me towards the middle of August when a large fish got off on a snag. Half an hour later the same fish took another bait and that proved to be a Delph best for me of 11lb 14oz. Adding a 9lb 14oz, another of 6lb and that 18lb pike made it a night to remember. However, the fish I caught were all rather thin and I was looking to catch a 13-pounder, a fish to beat my 12lb 13oz caught way back in 1970. Reading through the local paper I came across the story of a 13lb zander from another water. Now I had never seriously fished the drain in question, so it seemed a more interesting option to try a new venue. I went with Brian Hankins and as we walked over the flood-bank we walked straight into John Foster. He had recently been doing rather well with zander so it was a bit embarrassing to meet him hidden away here. Still my conscience was clear, having arrived at the same water by following my nose!

My first zander from the narrow water was 9lb 9oz which was soon followed by one or two others. It was a totally different drain from any that I had fished previously, being only 3 or 4ft deep, very muddy in colour and with reedmace growing out of the middle of the drain in places. The zander activity came either as it got dark or once in a while at dawn. Generally, however, everything came out during the night. Tactics were simpler than ever: a legered dead-bait with about 4 SSG to hold it in place, the drain being still most of the time. The Backbiters were set to full volume and I slept in between runs so that I could work the next day.

The next trip saw me move further up the drain. On small waters I am convinced that even light fishing pressure will force zander to take others with them. For this reason on the small waters I always try to keep moving. That night saw only one run at midnight on a typical starlit night. I have great faith in these conditions in summer, the drop in air temperature seems to get the larger zander to hunt a bit more. When I wound down to the fish it was a bit of a surprise to be met with solid resistance. While zander are not the world's greatest fighters they can give you a bit of a run around. Once in the net, you are still unable to estimate the size of a fish. That is, until you lift it. Then with the torch to illuminate it, I stood back for a second to take it in before unhooking the fish. In the dark a fish tends to look smaller than it really is but the tape measure told its tale: 34in long and without doubt a 13lb plus zander. Once weighed I realised that it had been worth waiting for, as she weighed 15lb 15oz! I put the fish in the water in the landing-net and fetched a young lad called Darren who was fishing further down the drain. With his help I took a few pictures and back she went.

The few days that followed were very special. At the time I had caught the third biggest zander from England and the second biggest pike! Needless to say that soon changed but it was nice while it lasted. The problem was I had done nothing special to catch that big fish; yet despite all my trying I was unable to better the 12lb 13oz fish caught sixteen years before. All this suggests to me is that luck does play a big part in angling and it does not matter how dedicated or how good you are, you still need a little luck.

Another factor which soon emerged after the capture of the big zander was the increased interest from other anglers. I have nothing against sharing my fishing with others who put the effort in, but there was no way I was going to put things onto a

If it wasn't bright and sunny they didn't feed

plate for the instant or part-time zander anglers! Because daylight fishing was not very good I started to arrive just before dark and leave at dawn. This had a useful bonus in that the anglers who were looking for me, missed me for over a year. In fact many thought I was on the Delph which was something I was happy to let them continue to think! With the zander fishing going so well, I had to put more effort in and I was often travelling down for just the one night. At the end of September I picked a 6lb 1oz up in the night and at dawn took a 12lb and a 7lb 10oz almost together. This had been one of the rare post-dawn periods of activity. All the large fish were in good condition and though I didn't have much hope of a bigger fish than the 15lb 15oz, any double-figure zander was a rare animal indeed and well worth working hard for.

By early October I had started to fish a paternostered live-bait as well as legered dead-baits. Earlier in the season trips with the live-bait proved a waste of time, so for a while I dropped the method. Not having to carry live-baits increased my walking range so that I could keep trying new areas. On the night of the 7th it was pouring with rain and I arrived just after dark. The live-baits outfished the dead-baits totally with another double of 10lb 12oz coming to the net.

By now the walking distances were getting a little out of hand but with a bit of chatting up I managed to get permission to use a small track to the drain. Again it was a windy night but this did not worry the fish. Before midnight five fish over 6lb had come out, the best weighing in at 9lb 6oz. Now this was zander fishing like the old days simply because I was catching the odd double for a change! November is just about the end of the season for zander fishing; however, the weather was mild so it seemed sensible to keep going. By now I had run out of new places to try so I moved back to where I had started and once again dropped lucky. The live-bait was accepted in the dark by a 14lb zander along with another of 6lb 1oz on dead-bait. To prove that this was a winning run a 31lb pike also hung itself onto my lure the same week. Though I kept fishing until December, eventually the really cold weather finished off the zander fishing. Still, having caught five zander over 10lb that season I was not about to complain. The end of the season bonanza never arrived so all thoughts were on what to do next season. On opening day I could go for carp, tench or zander. I chose zander, mainly because everyone else would be after carp and tench. A week's holiday would see me start with zander and make a quick switch to carp or tench, thus allowing the opening night shift to get back to work!

I drove down on the 15th and was all set up and ready to fish, just before dark. It was bright and sunny and all set to be a classic night. I couldn't resist casting out before the off and I had a run almost straight away. This I missed and one or two runs of a strange type came and went before, just as darkness fell, a proper run materialised. It was almost a repeat performance of the 15lb 15oz, except that this time I could see more. In the net was, without a doubt, a big one but not quite as big as before. Mind you a 15lb 3oz snapper is not to be sneezed at! A few more fish to 8lb 8oz followed that night and the next, then I went tench fishing. On looking at the pictures of the two 15lb plus zander it became clear that they were one and the same. The fact that the same fish almost certainly came out again at 14lb convinced me that the end was in sight. This is so often the case with zander. A population will remain undiscovered until something forces them to feed more recklessly. This is usually a decline in natural food stocks. I've seen this trend on many waters and the time to strike is when the zander first have an edge to their appetite. Leave it too long and the chance of a big one is gone.

My friend Dave Moore had, in the meantime, been busy elsewhere. The fact that his father had turned up a 10-pounder was good news and by now I was getting a bit bored with the same old stretch of drain. So the next visit was to a much larger venue where it was possible to cast 20yd without hitting the far bank. After a long walk, dodging the cow pats as I went, I arrived at the swim. There's nothing particularly interesting about this spot but over the years it has produced some good fish. In the Insulbag were a few bits of eel and some dead roach. The eel section on its day still remains the most versatile zander bait of all. It is ideal for long-range fishing and can be used again and again. The rod with the eel section was punched out about 60 or 70yd, while the other baits were fished closer in. I cannot remember when I caught the other fish of the session, an 8lb 10oz and 6lb 4oz, but I do know that the one I had long waited for from this particular water came just into darkness on the long range rod. It is so nice to get stuck into something very heavy at long range, even if it does want to do some knitting with the lines on the other rods!

After a long haul to the bank it was soon all over which shows that with long-range fishing you get a bit more action! She weighed 13lb exactly and was the cause of much wasted effort in later visits. It seemed as if it was a flash in the pan and was not to be repeated. We were later to understand that though there were some big zander in the water they were very thinly spread. If they could not be located in the known areas, then you had very little chance of contacting them. Finally I was forced back onto the small drain and though a few fish were about including a very thin 11lb

3oz, the prospects did not look particularly good. I tried a few new waters but generally I was making no progress at all. So instead of building on the results of last season it was a case of having to start again. The 1988 season was going to be a problem without doubt.

One of the biggest single problems facing you if you are fishing predominantly alone is that information is hard to come by. It is possible to compensate, simply by putting in much more fishing effort. However, now I had a young child, and a bait business as well as a full-time job, so I was stretching my resources a bit thin! Even though things looked bleak Dave Moore and I decided that we were going to carry on regardless. That June because there was less to get excited about I decided to start with carp. Four doubles to 27lb 2oz on opening day was more than enough to compensate me for Dave's opening day blank after zander! In fact the zander roadshow didn't get underway until the middle of July, such were the other distractions. Eventually I arrived in the Fens for an evening, night and morning session. I picked an out of the way spot that had produced zander for me in numbers as long ago as 1968. Luckily it had produced a few since then! But on this evening the zander indicated why this was a deserted spot: there were no zander there, either! I soon get bored by the total inactivity so I hiked back to the car and went looking for somewhere to park and fish. A quick drive down the bank took me to the first fence on the water and that determined the limit of my movement. I cast out and went to sleep but awoke with the feeling of intense nausea. I had obviously eaten something with an overload of salmonella.

Typically, while I was being sick a buzzer sounded and without any interest in the proceedings I hooked, landed, unhooked and weighed an 8lb 8oz zander. I recast and

then finished off what I was doing and went back to sleep. In the morning I felt much better and had a look around. There were fry in the margins all along the stretch and it was clear that this was attracting a fair number of zander. In subsequent trips I added a few more fish to 7lb 4oz but at no time did it look as if I was going to make a quick killing. There were one or two other anglers about and as a huge shoal of fish started to gather around the bridge it was soon clear that the zander were going to home in on this area for miles around. Sadly I had less fishing time than I had planned for and it was clear to me that I was destined to miss out when the fish did start to come out. Dave Moore went down for a couple of sessions and came back with an 8-pounder and even the local kids were catching doubles. I had a quick night session which started with an encouraging fish of 7lb 8oz on a paternoster live-bait. A little later, an 8½-pounder was followed, at last, by a fish which just scraped in at 10lb 1oz. Once again all the fish came once darkness had fallen, thus continuing that year's trend.

You can never be too certain about what the zander is going to do next. If we were to have some good old-fashioned floods with mild weather and coloured water then we could expect more daytime activity on some waters. There have, of course, been some big zander caught recently during the day but generally my own findings have been confirmed by many other anglers. Zander have super-efficient eyes and one wonders if water clarity has increased causing greater light penetration and making zander hunt more often at night. One thing is clear – all fish adapt their behaviour to suit their own needs. If zander find it easier to hunt at night, then this is when they will do it. No doubt in daylight hours zander will feed strongly if it is easier for them.

It is impossible to understand why zander change their behaviour so significantly. However, in the final reckoning, we do not have to know everything. All we need to do is to go out and fish as much as possible, put the jigsaw together and then hopefully catch zander!

12
A Decade of Johnsons' Tench
Chris Turnbull

In the shadow of the North Downs, amid the ugliness of an industrial area of Kent's Medway Valley, there lies a large spread of glistening gravel pits. One group of these waters has stood out for well over a decade as England's premier big-tench fishery. Although they never managed to produce a record for the species, they looked set to do so right up until Alan Wilson took his 12lb monster from Tring. What these waters did do, however, was to produce more 8 and 9lb beauties than any other water anywhere. They were also the home of a whole revolution in tench-fishing tactics.

Along with a few friends, I fished these waters throughout the eighties and experienced some of the finest tench fishing imaginable. However despite the high quality of this fishing, Johnsons has always managed to evade the media exposure given to other big-fish waters, so in this chapter I thought it time to tell our story of these lakes through the eighties.

Dawn on the stables swim

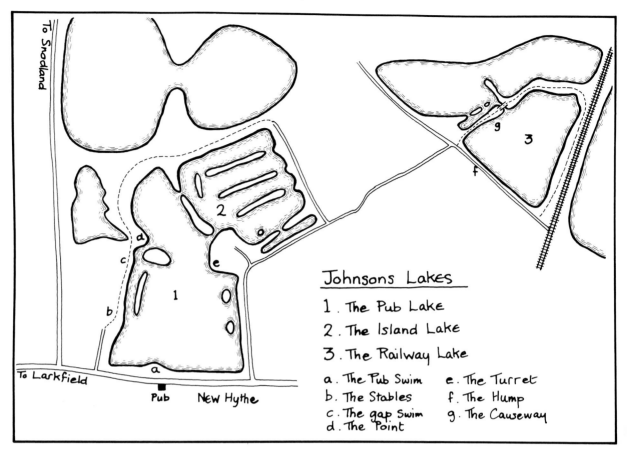

Johnsons Lakes

(map labels)

To Snodland

To Larkfield

Pub   New Hythe

Johnsons Lakes

1. The Pub Lake
2. The Island Lake
3. The Railway Lake

a. The Pub Swim
b. The Stables
c. The Gap Swim
d. The Point
e. The Turret
f. The Hump
g. The Causeway

Johnsons Lakes

It was back in the mid sixties when I first set eyes on the gravel pits of the Medway Valley in Kent. As an art student, newly enrolled into the Medway College of Art, I was travelling by bus from Maidstone to Rochester. From the top deck I looked out over the countryside as the sun slowly dropped in the western sky. As the bus climbed high along the side of the Downs, at a place known as Bluebell Hill, the view looked out over a large area of glistening waters a good distance off in the valley at a point where the landscape slopes off into the Weald of Kent.

In the dwindling light and the haze, the dark landscape contrasted sharply with the water's reflection of the last rays of the sun, creating the illusion of an idyllic scene. However, as my eyes adjusted to the light I quickly realised that the vision before me was not quite the picture of beauty I had imagined. Rather it was a landscape of mud with mountains of gravel and all the usual trappings of the gravel extraction industry. It would be many years before this myriad of pools would be fisheries worthy of attention. In the meantime I had my newly found independence to explore, a diploma to earn and the social life of the art school to get absorbed in, so for the first time in my life fishing took a back seat and the pools of the Medway Valley were forgotten.

It was some fourteen years later, early in November 1979, when I rediscovered those waters. After leaving art school I had moved away from Kent but now as a married man circumstances had brought me back to the county for a short nine-month period before we would be taking up permanent residence in Norfolk. By this time fishing had well and truly eaten its way back into my life and so within days of moving in, I was taking every opportunity to explore the potential of each of the blue dots on the map. Barely 5 miles to the north of our new home I could hardly miss the now well-matured expanse of gravel pits that I had first glimpsed so long before. They begged investigation.

The following afternoon I drove over for a closer look; apart from the inevitable pleasure anglers, it soon became apparent that carp fishing was the predominant activity in the valley. Slowly, through numerous conversations with many anglers, I started to build a picture of the potential of each fishery. One thing became obvious; few of these waters fell into the category of being easy. It was, in fact, several exploratory trips later before I saw any signs of activity other than motionless bobbins. It was on one of the smaller lakes, a pit of about 12 acres known as Johnsons Railway Lake. Two anglers fishing beside their parked vans seemed happy to tolerate my intrusion and were soon drawn into the inevitable line of conversation.

Like most anglers in the valley, their matching glass rods sat high up on the rests and converted Heron bite alarms, with red washing-up liquid bottle tops, hung as indicators on the lines. It never occurred to me that they might be fishing for anything other than carp, after all their set-up was identical to the others on the Kent carping

Chris Turnbull with an immaculate 9lb 7oz Railway Lake tench

scene. The older of the two anglers reeled in his rig to check the bait then after side-hooking a large brown boilie, recast 70yd or so out towards the middle of the pit. Minutes later a decent fish crashed noisily over the baited area. I wrongly assumed it had been a smallish carp but was politely corrected, it was a big tench. Suddenly one of the Herons blurted into life as the little red bobbin climbed confidently up into the rod-rings. Unfortunately the angler had strayed slightly from his rods and the bite was missed. This then was my introduction to Johnsons and its tench fishing revolution.

In the late seventies the angling world had been struggling to come to terms with an entirely new phenomenon in the specimen-hunting scene as it became apparent that tench were suddenly getting dramatically bigger. It had not been so very long ago when the Rev E. C. Alston's 7lb 1oz tench had, for many years, held the record and a tench of over 5lb was considered to be an exceptional specimen. Suddenly many waters throughout the South of England were beginning to produce 7lb plus fish, and the record was regularly being toppled.

Perhaps of all the new big tench waters Johnsons was the best, certainly it was quickly building the reputation as the most prolific. Five pound fish were very average, 6-pounders hardly turned a head, 'sevens' were caught regularly, 'eights' had become the targets and 9lb monsters were becoming a distinct possibility.

Johnsons can be considered to consist of three different pits, all of them capable of producing superb tench, along with carp up to the 'mid-thirties' and specimen fish of many other species. The Railway Lake, which I have already mentioned, is slightly separate from the other two, down a long track. The main two fisheries, which are actually joined by a narrow channel and a sunken bank, are the Island Lake, an island-strewn pool of perhaps 8 acres and the largest and most well known of the lakes, a water of probably 30 acres which is known by various names. In those days it was called the Boat Lake, but more recently it is referred to as the Road or the Pub Lake, due to its very close proximity to both the main access road and also the local watering hole.

Despite the fact that the complex lies in the shadow of a very picturesque area of the North Downs and despite being well matured, surrounded by willow, alders and tall poplar trees, it can by no stretch of the imagination be described as beautiful. The landscape is broken by large factories and warehouses and the pits are sandwiched between large housing estates and busy roads. There are tall industrial chimneys and a railway line runs alongside one of the pits. They sit amidst an area of scrubland, criss-crossed by dusty pitted tracks and electricity pylons. Worst of all, there is a litter problem, almost 100 per cent of which has been left by certain anglers who are a disgrace to our sport.

To the eyes of an angler, however, there is a beauty to be found at Johnsons which would remain unnoticed by the rest of the world. The water itself is a jewel, gin-clear, with a visibility of up to 12ft down. The surface is a mirror which reflects the blue sky with a pure richness. Being so clear, the water allows a view into the aquatic world in a way few pools can equal and it is possible to watch very big carp swimming in mid-water several yards out, or to distinguish groups of tench feeding along the bottom of the bankside shelf. The ph level is perfectly balanced to provide a rich diversity of aquatic life due to the alkaline-rich chalk aquifer in which they are dug. This richness encourages a profuse growth of aquatic plants allowing vast areas of milfoil to grow right up to the surface. They are the perfect big-fish environment.

Soon she is wallowing on the surface and rolls exhausted into the net

Being so late in the autumn when I first located Johnsons, I decided to wait until the following June before tackling the tench fishing. Due to the popularity of the Road Lake, I decided that when the time came, I would start my campaign on the Railway in the hope of catching a new personal best which after years of tench fishing stood at 5lb 4oz. It was, at the time, a fantastic fish and the biggest that had been landed by anyone during the three years that I had been fishing a canal in Devon from which it came. Compared with the potential of Johnsons, however, it was shrinking into insignificance.

By late May, I had plumbed the contours of the Road and Railway Lakes and by the beginning of June was heavily prebaiting my chosen swim with daily helpings of stewed wheat. Tench and carp were regularly seen in the swim and every day the bait was eaten. Due to other commitments I would be unable to put in long sessions but would have to make the best of regular morning and evening visits. On opening morning, June 1980, my goal was achieved with a pristine beauty of exactly 6lb hooked right under the rod tip in 6ft of water. By the end of that week I'd equalled it with a fish of exactly the same weight, plus taking a few 4- and 5-pounders and also a magnificent leather carp of 25lb 3oz.

Despite my success on the Railway, it quickly became apparent that some much larger tench were being landed from the Road Lake during opening week so now that the bivvies, which had occupied virtually every swim, were rapidly thinning out I decided to turn my attention to this water. Once again it would have to be short sessions rather than digging in. Along with my wife and daughter, I was due to move up to Norfolk the following week, so there was much packing to be done and arrangements to be made. Fishing time would be very limited indeed. This time I chose to concentrate on a swim which looked very promising but demanded a fairly long-range approach – its main feature being a long drop-off about 60yd out. Although Johnsons' tench were now well and truly weaned onto eating boilies, I had very little experience in modern carp methods at that time, so elected to use swimfeeders baited with corn and maggots. I couldn't go wrong and after two mornings and one evening session, I'd taken a string of good fish, nearly all over 5lb and topped with two real biggies of 7lb 10oz and 8lb exactly. I had fallen on tench fishing beyond my wildest dreams. Incredibly, now that I'd found it, it was time to leave it behind. Norfolk may well be the home of huge roach, chub, barbel and pike but no matter how good that would be, I knew I would be back to Johnsons, time after time in the future.

Over the following year or two, I made fairly regular visits to the Road Lake, at first on my own and later with a new friend, Norfolk angler, Jim Bigden. Like me, Jim had a deep fascination with tench fishing. Together, we started exploring the possibilities and benefits of adopting carp fishing baits and methods. Help and advice from new friends met at the water was slowly integrated into our approach. Paul Snepp, one of the lake's regulars, and Fred Wilton who regularly called in to drink our tea, were especially helpful and thought provoking. Slowly the numbers of big tench we were catching started to build up.

From the length of the fish we were catching, it quickly became obvious that their weight potential was colossal. We were witnessing spawned-out fish weighing up to 8lb 14oz. Nine-pounders, though rare, were beginning to turn up more frequently and as the national record was then still a shade over 10lb we rationalised that some of the 24–25in long fish of Johnsons could well break the record if caught in full spawn. With this in mind, we began to intensify our approach and started putting in far more time at the beginning of the season. As a result of this decision, during the opening days of the 84/85 season, Jim took an absolutely massive fish which at 25½in long, weighed 9lb 7oz.

During this time, the tench were absolute suckers for boilies. HNV baits would score well throughout the season but rubbish baits would catch just as many fish, providing the flavours were regularly changed. Straightforward confidence rigs, 18–24in hook links, tied with Dacron with 1in hairs tied off the eye, worked like a dream. Presentation was not so easy as the weed growth got denser year by year. Consequently many fish were lost during the fight despite the fact that few anglers ever used lines below 8lb breaking strain. Slowly, sadly and inevitably, the effects of this problem started to make its ugly mark on our beautiful tench; many were beginning to show the signs of constant pressure, torn lips from weeding up, split fins and line marks on their flanks.

Over the years, slowly the lake had become predictable as each season groups of fish

A new personal best tench weighing 9lb 11oz for Jim Bigden: his fifth Johnsons 'nine'

would turn up at the spawning sites. Mostly this was at a place known as the 'Gap Swim', a spot which Jim and I had really put in the limelight when he took from it the 9lb 7oz monster. Here they would spawn against the sunken willow roots on a submerged island to the left of the swim. During opening week or so, most of the fish caught would be pristine, immaculate creatures though there were the inevitable parrots amongst them. However, as the constant bombardment of boilies built up, week in, week out throughout the summer, many of the fish would stay in the swim. Oblivious to the dangers, their appetite for the little round balls of protein would keep them playing Russian roulette and getting regularly caught for their folly.

Being naturally an idealist by nature, this situation was not one that I felt at all happy about. There were (and still are) many beautiful, pristine tench in the lake; however, the number of damaged fish was really beginning to take the edge off my enjoyment of the otherwise fabulous fishing. Despite this, I felt that the lake owed me a real biggie, though I was beginning to doubt that the tench in the lake would ever grow to record proportions. No matter how long they grew, they just didn't seem to pack on the weight of spawn necessary to push them into double figures. It began to look as if 9½lb or so was the limit we could expect to catch them at: they were obviously losing most of their spawn before the opening week and it would take a bitterly cold spring to hold back spawning until late June or July.

Jim, Simon Lush, Paul Snepp and many other friends I had made at Johnsons had, by this time, taken numbers of 8lb plus tench; Paul had actually taken three over 9lb. For my own part, my first ever tench from the Road Lake had weighed 8lb exactly and though I'd since taken at least a dozen more over 7lb, anything bigger had totally eluded me. This injustice, I felt, needed correcting and so I decided to put in just one last opening week session on the lake before moving to pastures new.

Opening week 1986 and I was unable to get to the lake early to secure one of the few highly rated swims we had identified. I had travelled down overnight with another Norfolk angler, John Sadd. We arrived at the lake a little before dawn on 15 June and as we expected all the best swims were taken, so we would have to make do with the best of the rest.

After a brief look around the lake, I opted to set up in a highly unrated swim known as the Stables. This swim used to be a real winner, but in 1983 the water level had risen 6ft after pumping had stopped on a nearby pit. Since then the swim had died a total death and now it was totally overgrown from neglect. To the left of the swim, about 20yd out, a long sunken bar, covered in willow bushes, ran out 70yd up the lake to the Gap Swim. From experience I knew that the tench often patrolled along the back of the bar and also were likely to spawn on the sunken willow roots. Although they were never caught, I felt sure that I could make some sense of the situation and that the swim had real potential.

I elected to set up three rods. One, on the left, would be cast through a small gap in the willows and the bait drawn back to lie on the edge of an open gravel area hard up against the back of the bar. The middle rod would go tight up under the bushes at the end of the bar on a clean bed of sandy silt at the base of a thick milfoil patch. Both of these were tackled with 11lb Sylcast and 10lb Dacron hooklinks, harsh stuff for tench I know, but Johnsons' fish scrap like demons and with all those willow roots and milfoil to contend with, I would need every ounce of strength I could muster if I was to hussle these fish away from the bar quickly. The third rod was an easy option and would be fished on standard 6lb line tight under the rod tips in a clear gap in the milfoil in the

Sunrise on the Railway Lake

margins. Unlike the others which were baited with boilies, I decided to return to using corn on this rod, presenting two grains on a short 12oz hair with an 18in monofil hooklink, 1½oz bomb and backstop.

By midnight everything was ready, baits were cast to position and a handful of the little yellow grains dropped over the margin bait. Almost instantly I was in a deep slumber – I'd been awake for at least forty hours and was in real need of a few hours sleep. Twice during the night the optonic on the margin rod had peeped once or twice though the bobbin had not moved on the needle. Maybe line-bites, I had thought, or roach messing with the bait. Still knackered, I refused to take any real notice. It was just before dawn, and I was still out for the count, when suddenly the optonic on the same margin rod screamed out a totally different call to consciousness. The rod clattered in the rests and the reel handle spun like a wheel as I dived ungraciously out through the bivvy doorway. The rod hooped alarmingly as the fish bolted down into 10ft of weed-free water. The battle was powerful but brief as I hauled away blindly at the churning dark inky pool below me. In record time I had the still lively fish into the landing-net.

I was far from awake as I removed the size 8 hook from the back of the fish's mouth. The call of the bedchair was so great that I was tempted to return the fish without the bother of digging out my scales to weigh it, when slowly it dawned on my idle brain that this fish was a bit special. Suddenly everything took on a new significance, as on the Avons she weighed 9lb with a mere ½oz to spare. At long last I had overcome the bogey which for six years had prevented me from landing the really big lumps. That afternoon the tench spawned and to my knowledge no more 'nines' were taken that year from the Road Lake. As the man says: 'When yer luck's in, yer luck's in!' By the end of that week I'd taken a further ten fish over 5lb, including two very lean 7lb females and an absolutely massive male of 7lb 3oz. At the parting, I left the lake a very happy tench angler; my ambition had been achieved and now that it had, it was time to move on.

During the last six or seven years the Railway Lake had really started coming into form. Mostly it had been considered a big carp water but, although not easily caught, more and more big tench were showing up. It had produced a few 'nines' including one of 9lb 5oz to my good friend Pete Garvan and another friend Keith Ferguson actually took an enormous beasty of 10lb 1oz, the first double ever to be taken from the complex. Surely this fish was no fluke, there may even be bigger ones to be had, who knows? . . . There was only one way to find out and so with this in mind, I felt that with a slightly modified approach, different to those used by the carp lads, a few big tench might be taken.

It was to be a whole year later before I was to return to Johnsons. June 1987 eventually came around. The spring had by and large been a late and rather cold affair. The chances of the fish being spawned out were very low indeed, and we all felt that some very heavy tench were on the cards throughout the complex. John Sadd and I once again arrived just before daybreak on the morning of the 15th. As we walked around the Railway Lake in the darkness and the rain we noticed a fair amount of activity as a number of fish rolled regularly some 70yd out from the causeway which separates the pit from the more recently dug, Leisure Sport controlled Larkfield Pit. Other than this area of activity, very little evidence of fish was apparent elsewhere on the lake. Despite many of the swims being occupied by bivvies, the two beautiful swims which commanded this area were still free.

Like rats up a drainpipe, we shot in to secure them for ourselves. After erecting our bivvies and having a good civilised breakfast we set about work plumbing the depths and mapping the contours of the swim, an inflatable dinghy and echo sounder helping enormously here. Unlike the Road Lake, there are very few dominant features on the Railway, no islands and no shallow bars. The average depth is probably 16–17ft and the lake bed is a mass of small features, narrow bars, humps, bumps, plateaux, drop-offs and even deeper channels. From the surface none of this is evident and even worse the fish never stay in one spot for more than a day or so. These factors make the water a very hard nut to crack; it is a real challenge, but to be honest something of a lottery.

By midday we had our swim well charted: 70yd out from mine a long thin razor of a bar ran almost parallel to the bank. To my left, in John's swim, the same bar had widened out into an 11ft deep plateau before sliding off into a featureless expanse of water. Between us and the bar, the depth was a steady, equally featureless 14ft, and beyond the bar the bottom dropped off like a wall down to 17ft. The previous night's activity had been right over the bar itself. We rowed out and placed markers along the bar, one in front of me on an apparently weed-free hump on top of the bar. The other was placed in front of John's, smack in the middle of the plateau.

Remembering the success I'd had using stewed wheat when I first fished the water in 1980, we decided to feed the swim with the same bait and so once more the dinghy was taken out to deposit 2gal of wheat over a wide area which included both of our markers. On top of that little lot were placed two mixes of ultra spice-flavoured boilies.

Closer in, at the bottom of the marginal drop-off, I also elected to scatter a few pints of wheat and a few handfuls of boilies.

That evening I joined the other lads fishing on the complex, up the pub for a meal and a pre-season pint or four. The pub is the central point at Johnsons, hot meals, cold lagers, gossip, news and views can always be enjoyed, for many of us it provides a very necessary break from fishing. At 11.30pm the last car headlights bounced up the track as Steve Edwards, Oggy, Keith Ferguson, myself and the other members of the Bedchair Study Group made our way back to our swims. Soon enough midnight came around and throughout the complex, baits were cast out towards unseen markers. Then all becomes quiet and long hours pass by slowly before black turns to grey and dawn slowly awakens to reveal a bleak, damp day. Bobbins hang motionless as the kettle slowly warms on the little stove and so once again the long vigil that is big-fish angling has begun for another season.

The first day is something of a success and something of a failure, three takes come before breakfast and are well out of character for the Railway. One I miss completely, another, a tench, drops off after only a few seconds. Hooklengths are made longer and hairs shortened in the hope of solving this problem. Bite three results in a 21lb mirror carp, luckily I am almost as keen on carp as big tench.

In the afternoon the same baiting programme is followed. The rest of the day passes without incident. Dawn arrives on the 17th, another grey and somewhat wet affair. My beautiful swim is beginning to look a little worse for wear, the daisies and dandelions which had adorned the clean fresh grass are now squashed into the accumulating mud. I doze for a while, then recast the baits and return to the warm shelter of my canvas bivvy. For three hours all is quiet, few fish roll and few anglers stir. Obviously no one else feels inspired so I am surprised when suddenly one of my optonics splutters damply into life and the heavy bobbin gathers momentum as it slides ponderously up the needle. As the rod is struck and takes on its full $1\frac{1}{4}$lb battle curve, I feel that powerful deep chugging sensation pounding back through the rod which tells me that a tench is hooked. Slowly the rod is pulled down as unavoidably the fish turns off down the back of the bar, then all goes solid as my prize finds sanctuary in a bed of milfoil. This is the point at which most tench are lost, either in the weed or otherwise they fall off seconds after coming free.

I wind down hard and hold the pressure, 'Will she, won't she?' I ponder anxiously. Slowly I feel something beginning to give, then suddenly, gratefully, she is free. She moves off to my left, still behind the bar and now dragging my marker behind her. Although obviously a heavy fish, she seems to lack the speed and power which is the hallmark of most Johnsons' tench. Once drawn over the bar she just chugs away hugging the bottom as I slowly pump her the 70yd back to the waiting net. As I draw her up through the clear water, we watch as she works her great grey paddle and makes her last few dives for safety but it is futile and soon she is wallowing on the surface and rolls exhausted into the submerged net.

In the water we could easily see she was a big fish but now on the bank as I opened the folds of mesh I was taken by surprise by the size of her bulk. Although of only average length (being 22in) she was broader than any tench I had ever seen, she was carrying a very decent paunch of spawn for a Johnsons' fish. How big? . . . I could not guess, maybe even a double. The scales, however, were not as inclined to emotional exaggeration as my eyes and as far as they were concerned she weighed 9lb 8oz exactly and that was that. I wasn't complaining, I was in heaven.

There was no doubt now that my big tench jinx was well and truly broken. This realisation was confirmed by the string of big fish I took throughout the remainder of my two-week stint at the water. They weighed in order of capture: 6lb 7oz (a male); 8lb 7oz; 7lb 4oz; 8lb 5oz; 8lb 14oz. If these figures sound absurd, I agree they are, but to put things in perspective on two occasions I had to wait four days between bites; still, on the Railway even that's hyperactive!

After my 9lb 8oz fish, I think all of the tench lads were expecting to see a double come out as the fish had most certainly not spawned an ounce. However this was not to happen and most surprisingly mine was the only 'nine' the Railway produced throughout that season. On the Road Lake, however, 9-pounders were the order of the day. During the opening fortnight Jim took three, at 9lb 1oz, 9lb 2oz and 9lb 4oz, James Harwood had a monster and most probably a new lake record of 9lb 11oz. Dave Cable and Phil Wade from Eastbourne, both took fish of 9lb 2oz and Simon Lush actually managed to make tench fishing history by taking two 9lb 5oz and 9lb 1oz beauties both in the same morning. As if that wasn't enough, he also added another of 8lb 13oz and a 7lb 2oz male to the same bag.

The day before Simon's incredible catch I was enjoying a pint and a meal in the pub with a few other lads, each of whom had managed to take a 9-pounder at some time or another. Simon walked in, he bought a pint, ordered lunch and strolled over to join us; he had been struggling. As he went to sit down, he was politely informed that this table was reserved exclusively for the privileged few who had caught 'nines'. As he hadn't, he was told that he should go and find somewhere else to sit! . . .

The following lunchtime he strolled in again, on cloud nine. He bought his pint and walked over, looked down at us, then walked on past to sit at a vacant table. He had our attention and knew it. Looking over, he raised his glass and pronounced that his was 'the two "nines" on one morning' table! . . .

Postscript

Johnsons' tench seem to go from strength to strength, it may be slowly but I am sure they are still getting bigger although the vagaries of the British summer and the late spawning of 1987 and 1988 make it hard to tell.

In June 1988, I once again started the season on the Railway Lake; the fishing was harder than ever, but luckily I still managed a couple of biggies of 9lb 7oz and 8lb 9oz. Many anglers blanked, especially on the Road Lake; however, the average size was seemingly higher than ever for the few who caught. Weeks after my return, rumours filtered down the grapevine that both waters had produced doubles after the pressure was off.

The following season, the last of the decade, John, Jim and I returned for another opening week on the Railway which resulted in Jim landing a new personal best monster of 9lb 11oz. I fully expect these waters to produce at least another decade of big-tench fishing although they will get harder and harder, I am sure.

In the future, there will be many more waters which will produce big tench. It is open for guessing what their ultimate weight may become. One thing I do know is that however big the record may be, there will always be something very special about the long fighting leviathans of Johnsons which will never be upstaged by the spawn-bound or dropsy-ridden monstrosities which have too often stolen their limelight.

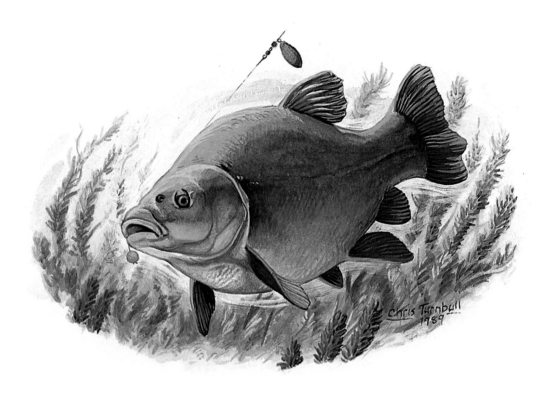

13

Savay: Queen of the Colne Valley

Andy Little

Throughout the eighties Savay has stood out as one of the most remarkable carp fisheries, for it is a fact that this beautiful water holds more 30lb plus carp than any known stillwater in the British Isles. Consequently Savay has drawn most of our very best carp anglers to try their luck; in fact, if all their names were listed together it would read as a 'Who's Who' in carp fishing today. One of the first men to turn his attention to Savay was Andy Little. In one season his catches were truly spectacular and surely beyond the expectations of any angler's wildest dreams. His results alone would have put Savay on the map as a fantastic carp fishery, and he only fished it for one season.

Andy is respected as an angler right at the very top of the carp-fishing ladder, and has a staggering number of huge carp to his credit. At the time of writing he is said to be fishing for his fiftieth 30-pounder; at that rate this number should be well out of date by the time this book is in print.

Andy has recently taken the jump into self-employment as an angling writer and tackle consultant. His writings have been published in many magazines, and he has written a very successful book on carp fishing; however, he is probably best known for his highly instructive weekly column in the Anglers Mail.

'From tiny acorns, mighty oaks do grow.' That is certainly true of Savay, the name synonymous with carp fishing today, which started its life as just an insignificant puddle of water. It was one of the many test diggings that were taking place around the 1930s. It was soon discovered that the area held rich seams of gravel, so more extensive excavation work was to follow.

The first organised fishing that took place at Savay was not carp fishing at all, for it was originally opened as a trout fishery. It was not until some twenty years later, when the Ruislip Club took over the fishing rights, that the first carp stockings took place. It was during the first year of its control in 1950 that the Club introduced three hundred carp of the Leney strain – what a significant stocking that was to prove! Now, with the benefit of hindsight, we have come to realise that, like good wine, carp also have their prime years and the 1950 stocking of Leneys was certainly placed in this category. So on reflection this was really the first seed to be sown on this water that has since become a mega carp fishery.

A year later the Club introduced a further three hundred of the same strain, creating a good foundation for future years. The Ruislip Club was formed in 1946, and its first water at Stockley Road near West Drayton was to become yet another carp water which has been the subject of great controversy over the years. It was extremely fortunate that it took over Savay in 1950, and managed it so efficiently.

It was in 1966 that I had my first insight into Savay, by pure coincidence. While I

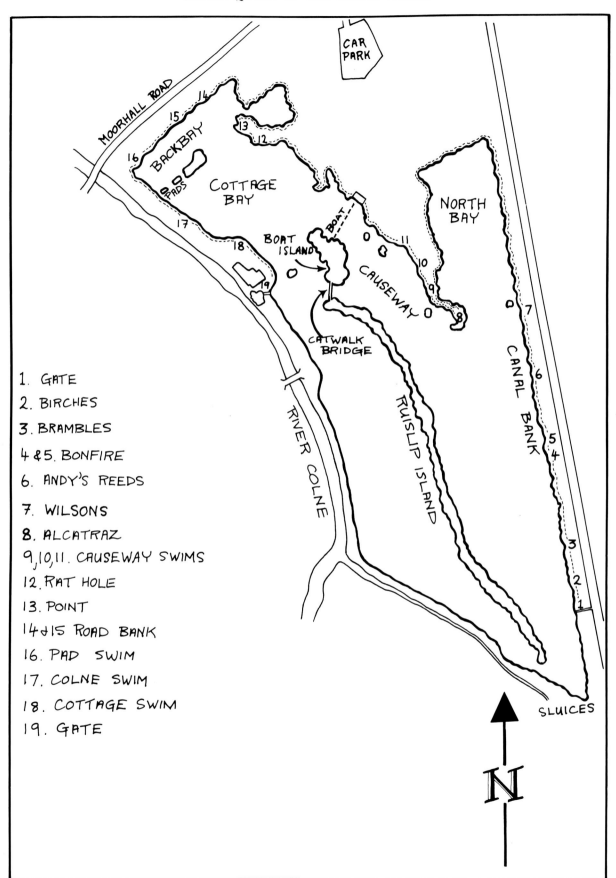

1. GATE
2. BIRCHES
3. BRAMBLES
4 & 5. BONFIRE
6. ANDY'S REEDS
7. WILSONS
8. ALCATRAZ
9, 10, 11. CAUSEWAY SWIMS
12. RAT HOLE
13. POINT
14 & 15 ROAD BANK
16. PAD SWIM
17. COLNE SWIM
18. COTTAGE SWIM
19. GATE

was being interviewed for the famous Wadhurst Syndicate by Alex Rennie, he showed me a picture of a three-carp catch that was taken around that time. The angler in the photograph was Cliff Glenton. This could not have been better, as Cliff ran a fishing tackle shop at Northfields Avenue in Ealing, very close to where my father worked. With a little probing here and there the location of that very good catch was eventually revealed – and, of course, it was Savay! I don't remember the size of those carp – they could have been large doubles or even twenties – but what I do know is that they were clearly printed on my mind forever. Even to this day I have no trouble clearly recalling that very significant photograph.

It was during the following ten years that Savay received the bulk of its stocking; there were literally hundreds of Dutch, Italian and Belgian strain fish introduced at regular intervals. Records show that by the end of 1976 there had in fact been a staggering 2,300 carp introduced into the water. It has to be said, though, that many of these were tiny fingerlings and the mortality rate had to be quite enormous, but naturally it still held a large head of carp.

In those early days the carp fishing that took place there was kept a closely guarded secret, with no more than about half-a-dozen specialist anglers fishing the water at any time. Amongst the successful anglers were Cliff Glenton, Alex Rennie, Mike Wilson and Roy Walsh. I remembered talking to Mike Wilson about Savay; he considered it to be a very hard water, and struggled with it for quite some time before it produced the goods.

It was around 1975 that two fairly new carp anglers, Terry Clarke and Gary Whitehorn, joined the Ruislip Club. Soon after that, at one of the early Carp Anglers Association meetings, Gary Whitehorn showed me photos of carp caught from an undisclosed Colne Valley Pit. Again, I knew this just *had* to be Savay! It is strange how events turn out for both Terry and Gary became my good friends and angling companions, even though at first they were very evasive about their carping activities.

The years between 1966 (when I caught my first glimpse of those Savay carp) and 1979 had flown by. I had served my carp-fishing apprenticeship on many varied waters and by the late seventies I was enjoying good catches on some of the North Kent gravel pits. This was where I met and came to know four very proficient carp anglers: Lennie Middleton, Kevin Maddocks, Keith Gillings and Bob Davis. These four, along with Paul Bray, fished as more or less a team with quite devastating results.

At the end of the 1979/80 season I was invited to be part of a small syndicate to fish Savay. Bob Davis organised the whole project along with Graham Rowles, the fishery manager for Redlands, who owned the water. As you can imagine, Bob did not have to ask me twice! The little snippets of information that had been drip-fed to me over the years had all come flooding back. Although I had not even seen Savay before I just *knew* it was going to be a very special water. Gravel extraction from Savay's conception in the 1930s had been extensive. For it was now a 65-acre, mature, prestigious fishery nestling in the Colne Valley amongst other gravel pits of varying shapes and size. Savay to me was then, and will always be, 'Queen of the Colne Valley'.

The idea of forming a syndicate was, believe it or not, to ascertain the potential of the carp fishing, so you can imagine what a marvellous job those early carp catches at Savay did for its image. At the time very few people knew exactly what was going on

Sally, the Savay common

134

there. I must admit to feeling sorry for those dedicated few; they were about to have their little piece of Heaven taken away from them, and it would certainly never be the same again. I suppose in the back of their minds all they could hope for was that the syndicate would fail, for everyone knew that it was a very hard water.

I found myself, with the other members of the syndicate, in a unique position, for as far as we could make out this was going to be a trial and may only have lasted for the one season. It seemed that the odds were stacked against us at that particular time, as there was a complete conflict of interests. On the one hand, Redlands wanted to make it into a viable, commercial fishery, and at the same time the carp anglers wanted to keep it as quiet as possible, jealously guarding this very special water. So in many respects it appeared to be destined to failure before it even had a chance to get off the ground.

Full credit has to go to Bob Davis for working away slavishly and trying to make it worthwhile. I remember him saying that we must keep a happy balance, we must catch carp and be seen to do so, but not so many that it causes a stampede. This sounds fine in theory, but was very difficult to put into practice. The syndicate was drawn up with twenty-nine members, consisting of some of the original Ruislip members, some local anglers and some known 'names' from around the country. These were split into two rotas on a weekly changeover basis, and when you look at the names of the members you realise that they just couldn't fail to catch carp!

Another magic moment: Andy with a brace of thirties from the Colne swim

Chris Turnbull 89.

Rota 1	Rota 2
Derek Cunnington	Paul Bray
Graham Marshall	John Richards
Andy Little	Bob Harper
Bob Davis	Tony Howes
Keith Gillings	Geoff Kemp
Lennie Middleton	Albert Rump
Kevin Maddocks	Bob Baker
Pete Ward	Roger Smith
M. Richardson	James McCulum
John Dunne	Sam Gates
D. Beckett	Keith Sellick
Mike Wilson	Paul Allen
Rod Hutchinson	Clive Deitrich
John Webb	Malcolm Winkworth
Graham McCulum	

I was fortunate enough to be on Rota 1, which meant we had first crack at the water. By now there was little left of the close season, and much work had to be done. I spent as many hours as I could on the banks of Savay, plumbing the depths and looking for fish. Once the season got started I had committed myself to fishing every available hour that I could, and I was lucky as I was owed quite a lot of holiday time. I also had the weekends, and as many nights as I could muster after work. I was so convinced that this was going to be a one off that I just had to make the effort and put the hours in.

Savay, in some respects, was a very daunting prospect – not so much the sheer size of the water, but with so many favourable areas it was very difficult to pinpoint more than one or two that were better than any other. From the close season observations it seemed that for most of the time the carp were split into two or three vast groups of fish.

I remember in particular one hot and sunny afternoon when a shoal of carp came directly beneath the tree where I was viewing the lake. There were so many fish in the shoal I couldn't actually count them accurately, but I would guess there were probably at the bare minimum seventy carp, most of which looked in excess of 20lb. A sight I shall never ever forget! It has often been said that Savay is a large water, and I suppose at 65 acres this could be true, but in the first year of syndicate we were not allowed to fish it all. The Ruislip Club still maintains some exclusive fishing both on the long island and on the Colne Bank, and I suppose all in all we probably had 40 to 45 acres in which to fish. The other lovely thing about Savay is that it is broken up by a multitude of islands, bays, lily pads etc. The syndicate was allowed to fish from the gate on the Colne Valley to the gate on the Canal Bank. Let's have a look at some of the swims that were fished in our first year.

Starting at the southerly end of the lake on the Canal Bank, the first swim was the Gate swim. This was the narrowest end of the lake, and directly in front of the angler was the end of a very long, thin island that split the lake in two. There was a nice bed of lily pads in the margins of the island, which was a good place to intercept the carp as they came down the narrow neck of the lake. To the left-hand side of the swim was the sunken island, which also produced its fair share of carp.

The next major swim along was the Silver Birches, and this was certainly one of the better swims on the lake. When a northerly wind blew up there was always a fight to get in this swim, and it was definitely a favourite of Rod Hutchinson. It had one amazing feature about half way out, where several bars joined together ending in dead-end troughs where massive amounts of food used to accumulate – an amazing hot spot!

Next to this was the Brambles swim, and this was definitely a through area. Carp could be picked up on their way to and from the sluices. Again, like most of Savay, it had a multitude of bars to choose from.

The next swim along was the Bonfire swim, in the widest part of the lake. Lennie Middleton and I had staggering catches from this particular pitch, where there were three main patrol routes: one of about 25yd, one of about 70yd and a third at 95yd. There always seemed to be a good chance of fish in this particular area, regardless of weather conditions. The nice thing about the Bonfire swim was that it was almost two swims in one, you could double up here and cover the same area.

Next was my favourite swim, which I created myself. I made a little gap in a large reed bed, just large enough to get a pair of rods through. This was a great stop-off point for the carp, and they would mill about for hours on end before deciding which direction to travel on. If a south or south-westerly was blowing they would either go into the North Bay or maybe travel up to the Cottage Bay, via the Causeway. Whichever they chose meant they had to come across the plateau, about 90yd out in front of the reedy little swim. This is where I had a marvellous start to the season.

Still going north along the Canal Bank I came across the best looking swim in the whole lake. This was Mike Wilson's, and not only did he turf it but he even laid duckboards down so you wouldn't get your feet muddy! Many hours of hard work had gone into constructing this swim, and it was from here that Mike eventually had some staggering catches. It was located just inside the neck of the North Bay and it had an extra attraction in the way of an island just to the right-hand side of the swim. From this island ran a predominant bar which petered out just to the left of the swim, which acted just like a funnel to carp coming in from the North Bay. This area was ideal for particle fishing which was Mike's forté, and most of his carp came in on flavoured maize.

In the first year of the syndicate, very little fishing took place in North Bay. There were certainly many occasions when there were carp present there, though more often than not they would have been intercepted before they got too far down into North Bay. There are a couple of huge beds of lily pads in North Bay which I believe have become very popular in recent years.

North Bay eventually leads out to a long peninsular known as Alcatraz. This was a really rocky, not very pretty, peninsular, which proved to be a very good vantage point, for at the end of Alcatraz the angler can look south towards the sluices, and it was very difficult for a fish to conceal itself from this point. Alcatraz never produced the sorts of goods that I thought it would do. In some respects it should have been one of the best swims on the lake, as such a vast amount of water could be covered from this pitch. However, it did produce a 30-pounder for Kevin Maddocks.

We now turn round and travel north again down the other side of the peninsular, an area known as the Causeway.

Between the northern end of the Long Island and a peninsular bank was a really snaggy area which was fantastic for intercepting fish travelling from the main part into Cottage Bay. But I managed to lose an awful lot of fish from here, so much so that I

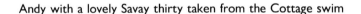

Andy with a lovely Savay thirty taken from the Cottage swim

stopped fishing the area altogether. The best session I had there was to land five carp out of nine takes, which was unusual for Savay because there were very few areas where you actually lost fish.

Next comes the Private Boat island, where the Ruislip boat was pulled across from the car park bank onto the island. From here via a catwalk bridge they could get to the long main island. Because of all the comings and goings around this area it was one that I did not fish, and it was unusual to see anyone round this particular spot. At this point the peninsular opened up into the Cottage Bay, another of my favourite areas. A strong south-westerly would see the carp moving into this bay in great numbers.

On the car park bank of the Cottage Bay there were two main swims, the Rat Hole and the Point. Rod Hutchinson fished both of these swims quite often and caught that beautiful 30lb leather that appears on the front cover of his first carp book from this area. The Rat Hole had a large canopy of trees above the swim giving very little overhead room for casting: you either had to get down on your knees, keeping the rod very low, or stand in the margins in a pair of waders. A lot of the Cottage Bay could be covered from this swim, and it was a very good vantage point.

The Point swim, which in fact was the exposed end of a gravel bar running between the car park bank and the Back Bay island, was one that I didn't fish much, although on odd occasions fish could be caught by casting tight to the island on either side of the bar. As we proceed round the footpath we now arrive at the Lagoon, which is another area that received little or no attention in that first season of the syndicate. In the past the entrance to the Lagoon (which is only a few rod lengths wide) had seen some good catches by Terry Clarke and Gary Whitehorn, using corn fished virtually under the rod tip.

Next comes the road bank. There were three main swims along here; the first two rarely got any attention, although I think the middle one may have produced the odd fish, but nothing of any real significance. Towards the end of the road bank was the Pad swim, which always seemed to produce carp almost regardless of weather conditions. I believe that they held up in this area for quite some time, almost becoming semi-resident. From the Pad swim you could place baits very tight to the edge of the large lily pad bed that grew between the islands, or alternatively the gap at the edge of the pad and island. This was a real heave-and-haul swim — not one for the fainthearted! Give them an inch too much and they were lost. Very occasionally you could get the carp going on surface baits, although personally I never had one off the top nor did I see one caught in this manner. Round the corner is the Cottage Road bank, which is an area that I believe is out of bounds now.

Along the road towards the cottage itself there are a couple of swims just either side of the lily pad islands. This was a very good area in which to get takes as you could easily intercept fish coming in and out of the pads. The problem here was that the angle between the bank, islands and pads was too acute for easy landing of the carp, so it attracted very little attention. The Cottage Road itself was flanked by a beautiful avenue of trees, and roughly halfway along this bank is the first truly fishable swim, known as the Colne swim. The path here was very narrow and you were almost set up on the Cottage Road. A similar sort of area could be covered from the Colne swim as the Rat Hole. This pitch was very good to me and I remember on one occasion catching two thirties on consecutive casts in less than an hour.

Twilight action in the Cottage swim

Leaving the Colne swim we come out onto a small peninsular which formed the main pitch in the Cottage Bay. This was my second favourite swim, not only because I caught an awful lot of fish from this spot but it was one of the prettiest parts of the lake. You had a panoramic view of the whole of the Cottage Bay, pads and island and it was very peaceful as very few people ventured round there. The beauty of the Cottage swim was that you could literally cover the whole of the Cottage Bay, and fish could be intercepted at any point as they ventured into this part of the pit. It was definitely a little piece of Heaven. The Cottage swim was really the last consistently fished swim on the Colne bank; although there were one or two more, they were not very productive. The channel between the Boat island and the Colne Bank was an area that the carp usually came through quite fast, rarely stopping to pick up any baits. It wasn't until they entered the Cottage Bay itself that they seemed to get their heads down.

I hope that will give you some idea of the type of areas that we fished in that first year. All were quite varied, and generally very dependent on weather conditions.

Although particles had been the killing bait previously I decided in that first year to go straight in on large, very hard boilies. There were a couple of reasons for this: firstly, most of the areas that I fancied would have to be fished at reasonably long range (from 60 to 90yd) as I firmly believed there were some extremely good interception areas both in front of the Reed swim on the Canal Bank and the Cottage swim on the River Colne bank, so with large, hard boilies I could naturally pre-bait these areas.

Secondly, I had a sneaky suspicion that the vast majority of the syndicate would be trying to fish particles – and why not indeed? They had worked well in the past, but I figured if I was to capitalise on the catches I would have to do something completely different from the rest, so it was an 'all or nothing' situation. I calculated that if I could get a huge patch of boilies out on these two major patrol routes I could hold the carp for quite a while. So I had a go; it was not unusual for me to spend as much as four hours catapulting bait out in order to create an instant dinner table for my quarry. Five thousand baits at a time was quite the norm, sometimes well in excess of this. Boy, did I get through some catapult elastic! In actual fact I always seemed to be running out and had to scrounge some off the other syndicate members.

I remember borrowing one of the new style whopper dropper catapults from Rod Hutchinson, one of the new all-singing-all-dancing-purpose-made pouches with latex bands. I remember him saying you won't break that, son! A couple of hours later, guess what? In the early part of that season I discovered the wrist rocket-type catapults, and what a Godsend that was. Mine was an American made marksman brand that John Richards had picked up for me, and it was a real revelation. I was only replacing elastics every other day – it saved me a fortune.

The baits themselves were fairly basic, with a high level of casein and flavoured with a high degree of maple. I found the best results were at levels round about 20ml/lb of bait, which is unheard of these days, although I think the concentrate level of the maple I was using at the time was fairly low. They were also sweetened to the hilt and glorious to eat. They were rolled up to about ¾in diameter which gave them enough weight to be catapulted 90 yards in favourable conditions.

I had another couple of aces up my sleeve; one was the hair rig which hadn't really got out at that time. I was privileged to be let in on the secret the previous winter, and what a difference it made to catches. Secondly, I was fishing pop-ups over these large bait areas and although today we very much take this method for granted, in the early eighties it was pretty much unexplored. Because most of my baitmaking was done on the bank squares of polystyrene were inserted into the hook baits before they were boiled.

Although it was obvious to all of the syndicate that this was a water with real potential, I was quite surprised how quickly most of them dropped by the wayside. This was great news for those of us who stayed the distance, as it meant the abandonment of the week-on-and-off rota system. So the scene was now set, and I used up most of my holiday in the early part of the season trying to be at Savay for the maximum amount of time. I did leave a week spare in case there was a flyer at the back end. As well as the holiday days I fished more or less every night after work and every weekend. Naturally, I had no family commitments at the time – I certainly wouldn't get away with it these days!

Every spare moment was used for making baits, and you can just imagine the vast amounts of ingredients I got through. A couple of months into the season money started to get a bit tight; travelling backwards and forwards, breakfasts in the café and the occasional meal at the Horse and Barge had certainly eaten into my savings. The bait was the first thing to suffer; out went the casein, and in came the semolina. By now the fish seemed to be so hooked on the flavour it didn't seem to matter anyway, and certainly there were no signs that it had affected the catches.

The lads who did stay the distance were certainly a great bunch and we all got on well. Lennie would turn up by train and stay for many weeks at a time. Rod would drive down, arriving with no food, bait or money and would usually try and find some work locally to pay his way. When the fishing was slow it would become quite sociable, and we would all congregate round someone's bivvy with guesting cups at the ready.

Daily calls to the Met Office sometimes prompted a midnight move in an attempt to beat both the carp and the other anglers to a desired spot. I recall passing one of the other syndicate members going in the opposite direction laden down with tackle, changing swims at the dead of night. I think we must have been listening to different weather forecasts – I'm not sure who got it right!

The fishing itself was often spectacular. Multiple catches of twenties, with the occasional thirty thrown in, were by no means unusual, although it has to be said that the lion's share of the fish really only came to three or four of us. The pressure was so intense, and we were so successful, that by November we had actually pushed the carp out of the syndicate area. They had been progressing along the Canal Bank for most of that month, and in the end it was only the Gate, the Silver Birches and the Brambles that were producing fish. It was obviously too much for them in the end, and they moved round behind the Ruislip island out of reach. This was really frustrating as you could see the carp crashing through the now sparsely leaved trees with no chance of getting the bait to them.

So it was on 10 November that I caught my last fish from Savay. I did go back for the odd weekend after November but did not manage to find any carp. When I look back the hours I put in were quite enormous. From 16 June to 10 November I caught forty-three Savay carp over 20lb. Thirteen of these were over the magic 30lb mark, the largest being 34lb 4oz, which I firmly believe was the largest fish in Savay at the time. I think this fish came out three times in all that season. It should have been Lennie Middleton's first thirty, but he foul-hooked it in the pectoral fin and did not count it, even though there were signs that it was originally hooked in the mouth, had come out and had taken hold again in the fin. There's an honest angler for you!

The irony of the whole thing is that although I had fished flat out because I thought this was going to be a one-off situation, I was then offered a place in the syndicate for the second year. I declined it, so the whole experiment had been a success. Although I was well pleased with what I had caught, one fish did evade me and that was the famous Sally the common which at the time was round the 27lb mark, the largest common at Savay. It was tempting to go back for another season just to catch this fish, but somehow I knew it would never be the same and in hindsight I'm glad I made that decision. The carp at Savay now have put on a lot of weight. Many of those fish that we were catching are now 10lb heavier, and I am sure that can be attributed to bait. I believe the carp at Savay in that first year of the syndicate had reached a free-wheeling part of their life when they were no longer naturally gaining in weight or length, and it was the influx of carp anglers at the pit with their good baits – a free unlimited supply of food – that induced this weight gain.

It would appear from the observations that I have made studying the press reports of captures at Savay that the carp are now starting to lose weight again, and it was only a matter of time before this happened. I'm sure they are now quite a bit more difficult to catch, have wised up to heavy baiting programmes and are more reliant on natural food for the main part of their diet. So I would not be surprised to see them returning to similar or maybe slightly bigger weights than we were catching in 1980.

I would have hated to have missed the wonderful opportunity of fishing Savay. It is one of my favourite waters, not only because it is a pretty place with large carp but because of the friends and memories it will always hold for me. Opportunities have come and gone for the chance to return. I have never taken any of them and probably never will. Maybe I'm afraid too much has changed.

14
Highs and Lows of Broadland's Glory

Chris Turnbull

Norfolk's River Thurne and its beautiful reed-fringed Broads have for many generations been famous for their huge pike potential. Indeed these waters have on no less than three different occasions provided anglers with record-breaking 40lb plus pike, as well as also producing another, which for various reasons was never accepted. Over the years this vast network of inland oceans has created so many angling legends for different generations of pikers.

In the eighties it emerged as one of Britain's major waters. Since the very first time I cast a bait on its water, I fell passionately in love with it both as a place and with the styles of fishing it requires. When tragedy struck the system in 1986, it broke not only the back of a legendary pike fishery but also the hearts of a generation of Broadland pike anglers. This chapter is the story of its monumental rise and devastating collapse as one of the finest pike fisheries of all time.

The history of the Thurne system of the Norfolk Broads is a long and fascinating one, spanning back far into the Middle Ages. Its pike fishing is legendary and surely warrants a book of its own to capture the wealth of stories that could be told. It would include the fabulous exploits of generations of Broadland pike fishers. Men like Jim Vincent, and his son Edwin and, of course, perhaps the greatest piker of all, Dennis Pye, a man who is reputed to have landed nearly 250 pike over 20lb. And what incredible pike they were, far from the obese trout reservoir fish we see so much of nowadays. For these Thurne pike are great long creatures with crocodile heads, truly wild leviathans which have ignited passions over many, many years.

Sadly such a book would also include many stories of great tragedy, for the Thurne is a troubled place, a vast watery paradise which exists constantly on fate's cruel knife-edge. The following excerpt taken with the kind permission of John Wilson from his book *Fishing in Norfolk and Suffolk* examines the decline of the Broads, especially the terrible problems on the Thurne.

The Upper Thurne system is still unique and like no other Broadland complex in that the water is all extremely shallow with a high saline content which enters through seepage and through land-drainage pumps via the salty marshes. Readings of 10 per cent have, in fact, been recorded in Horsey Mere. And it is in this saline environment that brine shrimps live, a valuable food source readily available to young roach, rudd and bream at every stage of their growth. I am convinced this is why everything grows so fast and so large in these broads, perhaps even the pike, which consequently never have a lack of the right-sized food throughout their lives from 3oz to 30-pounders.

Sport was also good on all the other broads, of course, particularly Barton for pike, bream and perch, and not forgetting Oulton for those truly giant perch. All the Bure-fed broads were also crammed with fish, but the fact remained that the Upper Thurne complex took the honours because it was outstanding.

To put a date on when the fishing actually first started to decline is impossible. There have been numerous localised setbacks in the last one hundred years, usually through the sea breaking through the defences at Horsey, affecting the Thurne-fed broads – something the sea has been doing for over two hundred years. In the late 1700s there were enormous fish kills caused by breaks in the sand-hills at Horsey with salt water covering the marshes for several miles inland. Since then, of course, acre by acre all over Broadland, swamps have been turned into rush marshes and marshes into grazing ground by banking up the tidal rivers and pumping water off the land. Steam and wind pumps were also used to free the marshes of regular rain floods but today, in so far as fishing is concerned, pumping water off the land is too effective by far. One look at the horrible 'orange' colour of Waxham Cut which runs into Horsey Mere tells the story. The thick suspension of iron oxide sediment simply covers everything and deters rooted plants from growing by cutting out the light they need.

Altogether there has been a tremendous decline of aquatic conditions in the Broads since World War II. In modern times, I suppose more happened to start a downhill trend in the late sixties than at any other time previously recorded taking Broadland as a whole. For starters, the algae *Prymnesium* hit the Upper Thurne system in 1969, decimating the entire stocks and putting to an end unquestionably the finest fishing in England, just a year after Horsey Mere had produced the record pike of 40lb 1oz to the rod of Peter Hancock. Incidentally, although *Prymnesium*, which releases a powerful toxin to interfere with fish's gills, struck so disastrously in 1969, it might have been responsible for fish kills as far back as 1911. Other outbreaks have occurred since in 1970, 1973, 1975, 1982 and 1984. In addition to the huge pike, specimen rudd, perch, bream and tench were also prolific in the Upper Thurne system, and all perished.

The 1969 *Prymnesium* bloom created a scene of total devastation which put the lid on the fishing of the Thurne while the following outbreaks in 1970, 1973 and 1975 banged in the nails. For the pike anglers of that tragic time, the system was finished; men like Dennis Pye and Edwin Vincent were to die long before any signs of recovery were to come about, while other anglers like Frank Wright, Reg Sandys and Bill Giles moved on to pastures new. The pike of the Thurne had become history, its broads were deserted and remained so for years to come.

Slowly but surely, however, a recovery started taking place and this was especially true on two small broads at the head of the river between Martham and Somerton. The first signs came unexpectedly, first in 1978 when a dead pike reputed to weigh 28lb was found at Somerton. It seems to have taken a while before the significance of this fish was fully realised, although a few of the Norfolk Grebes Specimen Group fished the area a few times; they only caught a few small jacks and decided the time was not yet right.

It was in 1982, when local angler Bill Florey finally tapped the full potential of the area with devastating results and is reputed in that season to have captured fifty-six pike over 20lb from the Martham Broads, the biggest of which weighed a full 37lb. Of course, Bill tried to keep his discovery under wraps but like all secrets the news trickled out and slowly, inevitably, others soon appeared on the scene. Yarmouth anglers John

The odd forgetful monster

Tipple and Paul Coull were soon in on the action, landing three 'thirties' up to 33lb along with several 'twenties' in a totally hectic one-day session. They also tried to conceal the location but couldn't resist reporting their great achievement to the press, so gave Hickling Broad as the water.

That summer, once again, the system had been in the news when A. Cotterell, a lucky boy of eleven years whilst on holiday on the Broads, took another huge fish of 37lb 8oz from the river at Somerton. By now it must have been obvious to anyone with half an interest in pike, that once again there were some very big fish around.

One man who had obviously cottoned on was Derrick Amies, a local man who had once regularly accompanied the late Dennis Pye in the sixties but who had given up piking after the *Prymnesium* kills at the end of the decade. Derrick had missed out on all the modern trends in pike conservation that the Pike Anglers Club was now popularising. Armed with the old methods, his Broads dumb-bell float, free-roaming live-baits, stout cane rod and gaff, he was now taking his old hunting grounds apart. Derrick's feats included landing six 'twenties' in a day and the capture of two 'thirties', including a monster of 36lb 6oz. Unfortunately, in keeping with the old ways, he killed both of the 'thirties' to be set up for posterity.

In 1983 a young angler Paul Belton who lived in the same village as Bill Florey, got news of Bill's 'thirty-seven'. Along with Dave Plummer who had recently moved to Norwich from Yorkshire, they decided to give Hickling a go in the mistaken belief that Bill had caught it there. Once on the system and looking around, it didn't take them long to put two and two together and arrive at Martham, where poor Bill was discovered moored out on the North Broad. Dave and Paul were soon entrenched in the finest pike fishing in England and their results were, of course, simply startling. Thirty-two 20lb plus fish fell to their rods including two whoppers to Paul from the South Broad which weighed 35lb 13oz and 34lb 12oz. The latter eventually grew on to become a new national record. In that first season Dave failed to get in amongst the really big pike but he made up for it in the following two years by taking three 'thirties' from the system.

Once this many individuals are fishing and catching on a water, no matter how quietly they go about it, the secret is bound to get out. The Thurne goldrush was now on, as many anglers flocked to get the chance of getting amongst the big-uns. Neville Fickling was fishing with Dave Plummer by then and was, of course, devastatingly successful, taking a number of 20lb plus fish including Paul's 34lb 12oz from the South Broad at night, this time at exactly 34lb. Eddy Turner and Bill Hancock were also getting in on the action, with Eddy catching the same 31lb 2oz fish twice in one month, once from the North Broad and once from the river.

The Norfolk Grebes Specimen Group members Martyn Page, Steve Harper, John Watson, Dave Humphries, Charley Bean and Steve Brown were now also getting amongst the big fish with several 'thirties' coming to Watto and to both of the Steves' rods. Other 'thirties' fell to the rods of John Wilson, Mike Davison and Ivan Leek. Not all of these fish were caught from the broads, however, as several came from the river nearby, including two real corkers from the Candle Dyke area – one, a massive 37lb 10oz to Peter Woodhouse and another of 34lb to an angler from Yarmouth. Despite this most of the angling pressure was heavily concentrated on the North and South Broads.

The problem was that both these broads were nature reserves managed by the Norfolk Naturalist Trust on behalf of the Nature Conservancy Council. The warden, Frank Pigg, was prepared to tolerate a minimal amount of fishing especially early and late in the day. It was important to the Trust, however, that the wildlife wasn't too frequently disturbed. Inevitably this was happening rather too regularly. During this time, a new warden, a local Somerton man Richard Starling, took over the post. Though far from being anti-angling, Richard was forced to take action if he was going to protect the Broads from the now regular intrusion of anglers. From his look-out spot in the remains of the old Somerton windmill he had a perfect vantage position to keep a vigilant eye on the Broads. From now on it would become almost impossible to get onto them as he would turn up in the warden's dinghy to evict the intruders. Obviously this situation couldn't carry on. Conflict was running high and as a consequence the South Broad, which was considered by the Trust as their 'jewel in the crown', was fenced off effectively from the river. As a compromise the Trust worked out an agreement with John Watson, Martyn Page, and Vic Bellars, the main committee of the PAC, and a system of limited access for pike anglers to fish the North Broad was drawn up. This system proved a great success both for the Trust and the anglers and has been upheld right up to this very day.

Once access to the Broads was brought under control, anglers were forced to search around the system more to try to locate a pike or two. On the river the fish took more finding but still the fishing could be highly rewarding for those in the right place at the right time. Big fish were still being taken periodically including a few 'thirties'. Norfolk Grebes man Steve Brown took three in one year, including a very determined lunker

Chris Turnbull poses with a real handful of twenties weighing 27lb 8oz and 23lb 2oz

which actually grabbed a half herring hanging over the edge of his boat while he attended his other rod.

Now that anglers were searching about more for their fish, other areas such as Candle Dyke, Heigham Sound and Deep Dyke were being explored. Horsey Mere, especially, was proving very promising. Derrick Amies had already put in a large amount of effort and was catching some very fine pike indeed. For reasons of his own, Derrick is wary of divulging the facts about his Horsey catches. However, few seasoned pikers will have forgotten the 41lb 8oz monster which he filed as a claim for the record, but which was refused as he failed to produce the fish as evidence. Some anglers remain sceptical of this capture; however, I doubt that many of the regulars to the Thurne at that time would query its feasibility. I, for one, would never doubt its authenticity or that of a number of 'thirties' which have since been taken.

Horsey wasn't the only place holding a few biggies as Yorkshire anglers Simon Lush and Wyndon Coole were to begin to find out. They were visiting the area following the reports of big fish from Hickling and like everyone else who had done so they were struggling like good 'uns. They were staying overnight downriver at Potter Heigham and after a week of blank sessions, decided to spend their last evening trotting live-baits on the river at Potter. Unexpectedly they pulled out a 'low twenty' of 22lb 2oz. On his next visit to the system, Simon pulled out another, this time weighing 19lb.

The following summer I met Simon at Johnsons while doing a week's tenching, and together we made plans to do a few days on the North Broad that winter. When the time arrived, the fishing proved rather poor with only a few low doubles and jacks. By mid-afternoon of the first day we decided to try a few hours at Potter. The area had no reputation for big pike, even though it was the major overwintering spot for the Thurne roach shoals. Mooring up opposite the big boatyards, we cast out a selection of live- and dead-baits and to my great surprise, didn't have too long to wait before Simon leaned into a 13-pounder.

The following day after a slow morning on the North Broad, it did not take us too long to decide we might be missing out on some action at Potter. After the half-hour boat journey downriver we were soon moored up and fishing the same spot as the previous evening. Very quickly Simon pulled out a small one and then an hour later, bent into a sluggish beauty which only woke up once in the landing-net. It weighed 27lb 9oz and was quickly followed up by one to me weighing 17lb. Obviously we had latched into something with great potential and so it proved.

The next morning we were back before dawn to explore the same area. Within an hour my paternostered crucian was snatched away under a moored cruiser in the jaws of a different fish weighing 27lb 8oz, which was soon followed by a 23lb 2oz to my second rod. I well remember our jubilation as we congratulated ourselves on discovering a new hotspot. I also remember our surprise when later that afternoon two pikers in a dinghy motored downriver to where we were fishing. I'm not sure which of the two parties was the most astonished. Cautious nods were passed but no other communication made. Later we learned that these anglers, Eddy Turner and Bill Hancock, had very recently taken a 29-pounder only a few hundred yards upriver. A week later we had confided with them, discovering that not only they but also Dave Plummer were on to this new discovery.

The following weekend Eddy was alone and fishing the spot which had produced to Simon and I. Meanwhile we set up 200yd upriver. For Eddy it was a red-letter day providing him with a superb brace of 27lb 5oz and 25lb 3oz. We photographed them in our swim and within minutes of returning it, Simon was away on a roach live-bait and duly landed an immaculate 28-pounder.

During Christmas week Dave's turn came and he boated two lumps, one was Eddy's twenty-seven, the other a superb 30lb 10oz. We were all set to keep the pressure on during the new year but unfortunately the gods had other ideas and the entire system froze solid and was unfishable for over a month. When it did thaw out, few anglers were on the system. I couldn't get out, but Simon once again was entrenched at Potter. He had plenty of action with several doubles but the big girls had vanished. Upriver at Martham, however, a far more spectacular event was about to happen. Neville was fishing from the bank a few hundred yards upriver from the Ferry. That morning a 49½in mammoth took his bait and made history when it weighed in at 41lb 6oz and toppled Hancock's old record which had stood for eighteen years. As if that fish wasn't enough he followed it the following day with another of 32lb.

Suddenly the Thurne was the place to be as pikers from all over the country converged on its banks. Very few were to be successful, however, as very quickly the fish disappeared to the quiet and protected places, away from the pressure.

When the 85/86 season came around, it opened on a tragic scene on the Thurne. Once again *Prymnesium* had raised its ugly head. It was the largest known bloom recorded in the history of the system. Luckily, occurring in the spring as it did, thousands of fish were still on the rivers rather than on the broads where they would gather to spawn. A mass exodus of bream and roach fled the scene by moving downriver to find sanctuary on the Bure. The pike however, once again, had fallen foul of *Prymnesium* toxins and throughout the system many of them perished. Horsey especially was devastated. At Martham many pike died, but one or two pockets of water on the river were not so badly affected and numerous fish moved into them.

A few opportunist anglers were making the most of this situation mostly by night fishing from the bank after the activity of the cruisers had quietened down and several good fish were taken. Derrick Amies was one of the anglers who had found a *Prymnesium*-free pocket on the river. From it both he and Dave Plummer had recently taken a 'thirty' each. On the 23 August they were sharing a boat together in the almost certain hope of another biggie, I doubt that they were aware that history was once again in the making. At 6.15am Derrick's free-roaming roach live-bait was grabbed by the same 'forty' as had blessed Neville. This time it pulled the scales around even further and was eventually accepted at 42lb 2oz, raising the record once again.

The piking on the river between Somerton and Martham was spectacular that winter as it was on the North Broad. Many big fish were landed including a 30lb 1oz to Martyn Page and not a few repeat captures of the 'forty' at a slightly lower weight, which had now been given the name of 'Dora'. Another biggie, in fact Martyn's 'thirty' was later caught down at Potter Heigham by Richard Furlong; this time it weighed 34lb 12oz. The fishing pressure by now was very intense and many fish died as a result. In response, most of the remaining pike disappeared to escape from the hassle probably to take up permanent residence in the sanctuary of the South Broad.

Today, the Thurne is once again a quiet place. Pike anglers are few and far between and the pressure is off. Occasionally a big fish is turned up, maybe on the river, occasionally on the North Broad having come out of hiding. A few more have been taken by the hungry few who are prepared to break the rules and poach the South Broad. For the vast majority, however, the South Broad is now respected as out of bounds; it is a place which we would love to fish but where the few 'kippers' which have survived *Prymnesium* and the boom time are free to live in peace and propagate new generations which, God willing, may once again spread out through the system.

We are prepared to leave them to it but outside that special place, throughout the rest of the Upper Thurne, I for one will remain guiding my boat ever-searching for the odd forgetful monster should it stray to where my baits are working. For me, no matter how hard it can be, the Thurne is still a magic place and like Yates at Redmire, it has captured my soul.

15
River Thurne Pike
Neville Fickling

In the early eighties Neville Fickling, a young pike fishing fanatic of almost legendary status, turned his attention to the Thurne system with staggering results. Not only did he land a new record for the species, plus a vast tally of 20 and 30lb specimens, but also he confirmed his place as the most successful living pike angler of the day. Few anglers have a deeper knowledge of the Thurne or could be considered more qualified to write this chapter. In its pages, he guides the reader through this fantastic system of waters, broad by broad, down its river and along its dykes, in honest and often hard-hitting detail.

Neville is a prolific angling writer, who apart from regularly contributing to both weekly and monthly publications, is also the author of two very successful books on predator fishing.

Time continues to pass by and yet another chapter in my pike-fishing life fades into the distance. From time to time I still go back and fish on the Thurne but, in reality, without being able to mount a long-term campaign I've been unable to become attuned to the water again. To catch consistently the Thurne is a water you have to concentrate on. It does not respond to half-hearted efforts or attention that is split

Chris Turnbull 89.

Autumn action on the North Broad

between a variety of venues. So much of what I am about to write here is based on those heady days of the early eighties when pike-fishing history took a bit of a jolt as one big catch followed another and hit the headlines.

The Thurne presents two faces to the angler. One is the romantic side: Arthur Ransome's Coot Club and Big Six; the legendary anglers of the past; the beauty of the place in the winter and the crossing of paths with the handful of people who take an active interest in the natural beauty of the area. The other face is hard and cynical: the motor cruisers, the holiday homes and, of course, the pollution. In between the two faces is the reality that is the River Thurne. As far as unspoilt beauty is concerned, the Thurne has little to offer compared with the wild lochs of Scotland and Ireland. Anything manmade tends to lack that essential feel of the wild. Yet the pike angler has more to concern him than just his surroundings. While it is preferable to fish where the surroundings are nice, sometimes the pike angler has to go where the drive for big fish takes him. The Thurne system is such a place and it is unlikely that there is any fishery in the country, save those waters with limited access or which cannot be fished, which has the potential for big pike, ie 35lb plus fish. For that, without doubt, is the sort of fish that has driven many anglers to make great efforts to fish this system.

When the words Thurne system are used, most anglers think of one thing, Martham Broad, yet the Thurne system is much more than just this. There are a number of large sheets of water connecting rivers or dykes. To give the reader some understanding of the Thurne it is worth describing the whole system bit by bit. The River Thurne itself starts at the village of Somerton as a dead-end cut, though a variety of small dykes are pumped into it. As far as the term river is concerned it is debatable whether or not the Thurne, in this area, deserves such a title! From Somerton to Martham Broad the river is only 4–6ft deep and most of it is very heavily weeded. Marestail and a variety of potamogetons predominate to form a dense carpet of weed which is sufficient to hide even very big fish. At Somerton the river is perhaps 10yd wide, but by the time it has reached Martham Broad it is 20yd in width. If you are looking for features then forget it! One bend and a continuous line of reed-beds is about it! Yet in 1986 when *Prymnesium* struck again, the pike were forced out of the broads and onto the river. At the top of the river some fresh water came in and because of this huge numbers of big pike were packed in. The morality of fishing for fish which are in distress remains to be considered. However, it is clear that if this ever happens again the area should be declared a no-go area so that the pike have a chance. Being caught might encourage them to try and leave the area with fatal consequences.

Neville's dream: his 41lb 6oz ex-record pike

The two Martham Broads are similar in many ways. The South Broad is connected to the river, but cannot be fished, while the North Broad is fished and is much more a part of the river itself. The South Broad is 4–6ft deep, with dense beds of marestail and chara (stonewort), a peculiar type of macro-algae. The reeds come right to the water's edge with undercut banks in some places. This broad along with the North Broad is the home of many of the Thurne pike. They are super hotspots. Now hotspots have been noted on many waters and these are without doubt areas where pike like to spend much of their resting time. They will feed within the hotspot but generally move out to hunt and this is often over a large area. In my opinion, both the Martham Broads have acted as hotspots, with the pike leaving them from time to time to hunt on the main river. This means that the same pike which are caught on the broads can be caught from the river. Unfortunately experience has shown that catching the pike from the river is twenty times harder than catching them from the broads themselves. The salinity on Martham Broads can sometimes be quite high and it is common to see lots of the small shrimp which are happy in brackish water. These shrimps undoubtedly provide an excellent food supply for many of the Thurne roach, rudd, perch and bream, perhaps helping the food chain which inevitably leads to the pike in the end.

The peculiar thing about marestail is that it continues to grow throughout the year. So if you fish these broads in February do not expect to find the weed dead and gone! In summer marestail has an emergent phase and during this stage it actually grows out of the water. Some readers will remember Fred Wagstaffe's adventures on the Thurne system and many of the pictures of that time had emergent stems of marestail in the picture. Pike, without a doubt, like this weed and can use it for cover and ambush tactics. On other waters where it grows in profusion I have actually seen 20lb pike sitting in the middle of gaps in it! The Martham Broads are also noted for the odd rare aquatic plant, one of which is called *nais*. This small green plant is a sort of cross between a succulent plant and holly. It is certainly unmistakable and grows in large amounts in some areas of the North Broad.

Water flowing into and out of these broads can be substantial with as much as a 2ft rise and fall due to the tidal nature of the river. It is said that low water levels can concentrate the fish in the deeper areas, though I have not noticed this myself. Leading out of the North Broad the river winds round a series of bends past Dungeon Corner into a long, almost straight, section which leads down to the Ferry. The river soon widens out again to its full width after the bends and until you get to the large tree on the south bank the weed is profuse. Then abruptly the weed is gone and the river is almost bare down to the Ferry and Martham Pit. A lot of fish have been caught from the stretch of river from the corner to the Ferry but the frustrating thing is that they are not always there. When the pike have moved onto the river, they can be anywhere in the weedy section or the barren area. It is very much a case of finding out the hard way. Downriver of the Ferry, the riverside homes start and for nearly a mile to the junction with Candle Dyke, the river is singularly uninspiring. Candle Dyke is itself where the Thurne starts to flow more quickly. It is also about 30yd wide and varies from reed-lined banks to residential housing. Right down to Potter Heigham it is a barren piece of water, yet over the years some big pike have come from it. The same applies to Candle Dyke Corner. There seems no way of predicting the pikes' presence in this part

The Upper Thurne and its broads

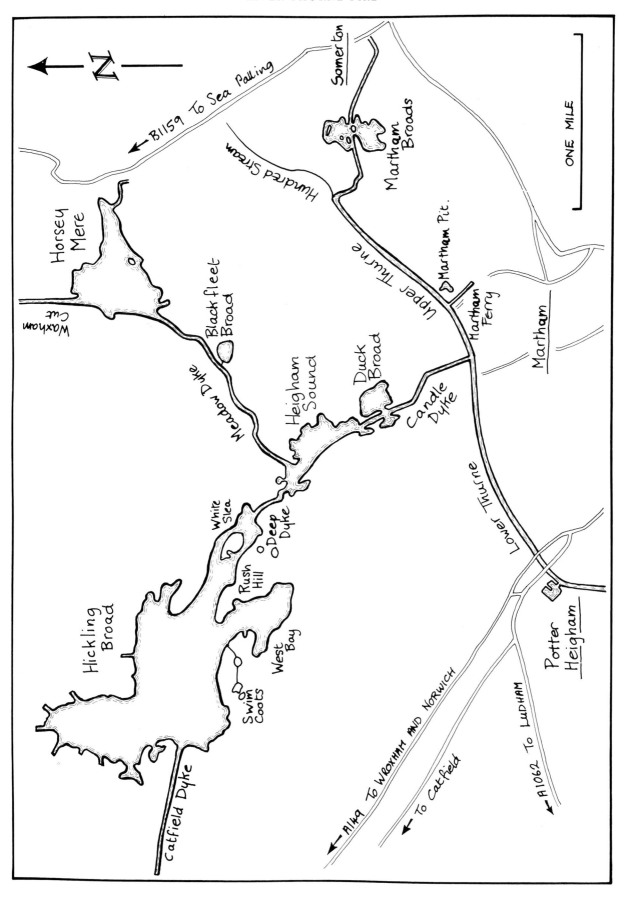

of the river yet, year in year out, the occasional big fish keeps turning up. No one knows, for sure, whether the big pike on the lower river are resident, or from Martham or Heigham Sound. My guess is that the pike are a mixture of the three and this is the one reason why they are so difficult to come to grips with. Each stock has slightly different habits and because there are only a few of them it is nearly impossible to make head or tail of what's going on!

For some anglers, Potter Heigham is the only place on the Thurne. This is probably because of the congregation of roach in the area in the winter – the boatyards are packed with them. The pike can turn up for a few weeks and then they are off again. There seems little you can do but to fish the area and hope you are there when the pike arrive. The area between the two bridges and the entrance to the boatyard is popular but full of snags. Here straight legering is not advisable. Beyond Potter Heigham to the confluence with the Bure is an unknown quantity to me, at least. I suspect that pike do exist down there, but the rest of the Thurne is a big enough problem without looking for more.

If you turn left at Candle Dyke Junction on your way back up the river you will follow another wide channel which eventually opens up into Heigham Sound. This length of Candle Dyke is an absolute pig and has defeated most people including myself. One 8-pounder is my sum total for several days' effort.

Heigham Sound itself is little better for it is here that the effects of *Prymnesium* begin to be felt most often. While the roach, rudd and bream seem to survive in large numbers, pike seem to have great difficulty in avoiding the killer algae and its deadly toxin. It is said that pike are slow to move away from areas with a build-up of toxin. While many of the prey fish species are quick to leave the area, the pike seem all too frequently to get caught, suffering the inevitable consequences. Yet Heigham Sound, for all its lack of pike, seems to make up for it with some big fish. The truth of what may or may not have been caught there in recent years is unclear. However, so many rumours of the odd very big fish lead us to one conclusion: there is no smoke without fire! Heigham Sound does offer some variety in habitat. There are some big weed-beds and odd bays with variable depths. Then there is the large shallow Duck Broad which is interesting, but not productive! I remember sitting there one windy evening watching bream after bream rolling in the water. No pike showed though! Mind you the amount of effort I have been able to devote to both Heigham Sound and Duck Broad proves nothing at all. I dare say someone, one day, will drop onto a very big fish. For that is the stuff of dreams!

Moving up further and turning left is Deep Dyke, the scene of capture of some big fish during the sixties. This area holds some big shoals of bream in the summer and pike to at least 15lb have been caught here in recent years. Further up still is Hickling Broad, the supposed scene of capture of many of the big pike in recent years. I would be very surprised if any of the big pike reported came from there! Hickling, at times, is alive with small roach, yet as far as pike are concerned it is an impossibly hard water. Of course, there must be some there, but the best of luck to anyone who has the nerve to fish it seriously. Because it is a big water, the wind can make it pretty rough and it is not the place to take a very small boat. My experience on this water can be summed up in two trips and one word . . . blank!

The right-hand fork, Meadow Dyke, winds its way east to perhaps the most famous

The beauty of the place in winter

of Norfolk Broads, Horsey Mere. Opinions vary as to its size – I reckon it's around 100 acres. Nowhere deeper than 7ft Horsey Mere was once the best pike water in the country. From time to time it still shows a little of its old form, but once again *Prymnesium* is suppressing the pike population to a rock-bottom low level. Somehow some pike always survive but these fish are greatly outnumbered by the rudd and roach which abound there. They are easily caught on rod and line wherever you fish on the mere; if only it were so for the pike! Another factor making it difficult to catch pike on this water is the fact that from 1 November to the end of February the water is closed to boat traffic including anglers. Add to this the heavy boat traffic when it is open in the summer and autumn and it is clear that the angler is up against it. Yet despite this, each season pike are caught. They are not always huge fish, but any pike from Horsey counts in my book. The mere is very weedy in places with plenty of marestail and milfoil to cast into! The colour of the water varies depending on the amount of algae and iron-stained water being pumped into it. At certain times the water is quite orange but this is no cause to worry as the pike have long become used to feeding in these conditions.

To my mind on Horsey the biggest single problem is boat traffic – the pike certainly try and keep out of the way of the milling cruisers and sailing boats. There are quiet corners here and there, but find one and some idiot will decide to windsurf through it! That then concludes the potted guide to pike fishing on the Thurne system. It is all very well knowing the potential of each water, but without knowing the when and how to fish them, you will not get very far. It would be pretentious of me to suggest that I know exactly how to tackle the entire system. There has not yet been an angler who has been able to come to grips consistently with the Thurne as it is now. No single method and no single area can produce consistent sport. It is a case of throwing everything you have into your campaign and hoping for a little luck.

The first useful assumption to make as regards Thurne pike is that they prefer to get out of the way of boat traffic. This means that they can be found where boats have no access. Some of the very private broads such as Martham South Broad come into this category. Without doubt many of the Upper Thurne pike spend much of their time out of the way there. There are two ways of tackling this problem, one is to poach the water, the other is to wait until the pike come out. Now poaching is in many ways the easy option but the problem is that once one person does it, everyone wants a go. Inevitably this would cause serious problems and in the end things would be changed so that poaching was impossible. It is far better for all concerned, and this includes the pike, to wait until the right conditions prevail and those pike come out. A very cold period certainly seems to do this with fish showing on the main river in areas where once before there appeared to be no fish at all. However, fish from that broad have turned up out of the blue on the river and it certainly pays to keep the fishing effort going if you want any chance of a really big one. The North Broad also holds some good fish but, because it is fished, they frequently wander away from the broad turning up on the river. Since the last *Prymnesium* outbreak, very few 'thirties' have come from the North Broad. Maybe they will come back again before long.

Another assumption which has generally proved to be true when I've been fishing on the Thurne is that if you can get a bait near a Thurne pike you will catch it. They are very opportunist feeders and will soon jump on a live- or dead-bait if, of course, you manage to find them! Most Thurne pike are fairly long fish which tends to indicate that they are fairly old. I am sure that the Thurne pike manage to get plenty of easy

Dave Plummer's best, a Thurne beauty weighing 31lb 6oz

feeding in the spring and summer while the other fish are spawning. However, once these fish have moved off to their winter quarters, often on the rivers, the pike have a harder time of it and this means that they will frequently have a go at any bait chucked at them. You therefore do not need to be a genius to catch Thurne pike, though being a lucky genius might help . . .

Probably the most reliable method on the Thurne system is the humble legered dead-bait. In the old days the legered herring certainly took its share of the pike. Either straight legered or with a float for bite indication the legered dead-bait continues today to catch a large proportion of Thurne pike. Your choice of bait is somewhat arbitrary because big fish have been caught on most of the common baits. Of my four Thurne 'thirties' one fell to a smelt, one to a float paternostered herring head and one to a legered herring. One fish came to live-bait and that accepted a roach of about 8oz paternostered close to baits such as half mackerel as well as those already mentioned. Wobbled dead-baits have also played a part. Though dead-baits have been very successful it is a foolish angler who does not have some live-baits with him. I have known days and whole periods when dead-baits have been ignored, yet live-baits have produced several fish, thus averting what could have been a disaster. Some anglers are put off by the prospect of casting a dead-bait into thick weed, yet the pike seem happy enough to pick them up there. Personally I will always try to put a dead-bait into a clear area or suspend it just off the bottom under a float. Fished on a paternoster, dead-baits can be highly effective. Other anglers simply insert polystyrene or balsa inserts into their baits.

Wobbled dead-baits are best fished without any weight at all and allowed to skip along just over the weed. Takes on baits fished in this manner are obvious to say the least. I have found that wobbled dead-baits only work well where there are a few pike. On the really hard waters, it is such hard work and so many baits are used without result. It is more sensible to use other more relaxing methods.

Live-baits have always produced pike on the Thurne system and perhaps the best known approach is the shallow float-fished live-bait. Small baits work best for me using this approach simply because in dense weed a big bait soon finds its way into it. Larger baits up to 8oz do tend to evoke a better response from big pike but these days about 4oz is as big as I'm prepared to go for this technique.

If you are prepared to work hard with live-baits it is sometimes possible to evoke a response from a pike which might not be hungry. However, to fish a free-swimming live-bait does require total concentration and this is difficult when you are trying to fish other rods with dead-baits. A float paternoster rig is the answer in many areas where the weed growth is minimal or non-existent, but in the real jungle swims it does not work at all well. Where there is some weed a long paternoster tail can allow the bait to fish unhindered above the weed. On the main river where there is no weed the paternostered live-bait remains a standard presentation.

Though the methods are relatively straightforward, getting to grips with the weather conditions is a totally different problem. I have found that a hard frost tends to kill things stone dead, especially in the morning. Luckily some sort of response can be had from the pike later in the day and sometimes dusk can be the witching hour. I well remember one day that dawned sharp, bright and cold and the river seemed totally dead. I worked along in the boat trying new areas until it was quite bright and warm. Then out of the blue the only run of the day came on a live-bait, a most welcome 24-pounder. This is one reason for always fishing a live-bait, for on the difficult days a bait which has a bit of life in it can make all the difference.

The key to Thurne pike is wind, they certainly feed well in windy conditions and many of my best fish have come on those days when the rod rests have been set low and angled into the wind. Even bitterly cold days when the sun was out, yet water froze in the bait bucket, have been productive with one fish of just over 20lb coming in these conditions. The now blatantly obvious long freeze-up followed by a mild windy spell is also something that has to be capitalised on when it finally comes along. Sadly in the winter of 1988–9 it did not happen and many anglers fishing a variety of waters found things very hard going because of an unusually mild winter.

Strong east winds can cause salt tides which surge into the river and can spread up as far as Candle Dyke. This can make much of the river unfishable but should, in theory, concentrate the pike. When I fished to this formula I did not catch anything at all! It may be that the salt influx puts the pike off the feed altogether.

Night fishing is another useful trick to have up your sleeve. I'm not a believer in sitting on a swim for weeks on end in a bivvy but when you are fishing a weekend and the weather is nice, it is just as easy to fish during the night as well as the day. Most of my night-caught pike on the Thurne have been doubles with a couple of fish over 20lb. One pike certainly was active at night with an air temperature of minus 7°C for it scoffed my sardine along with a whole live eel which must have been passing by earlier!

The future of Thurne pike fishing hangs in the balance, much as it always has done. *Prymnesium*, salt tides, poor angling technique and eel netsmen have all contributed to a decline in the pike population. Anglian Water did stock some small fish which may well serve to help in the future. However the Pike Anglers Club continues to press for an experimental introduction of tagged pike to waters such as Horsey in order to see if restocking with pike has a beneficial effect on the fishing. This is the sort of work that has to be done particularly if a pike population is really up against it. A slow trickle of modest-sized fish ought to increase the survival of pike, which once they get above a few pounds seem more able to get away from *Prymnesium*-affected areas.

Marsh Harrier
Chris Turnbull 89

The only plus point with poor pike survival is that the average size of the surviving pike can be very high. However, waters such as Horsey can support a lot of big pike, with the odd fish of 40lb, such as Hancock's fish of 1967. Ultimately we need to see an end to saline water being pumped into the Thurne along with the nutrients that promote algal blooms. I fear that on the present performance of those involved we may have a long, long wait.

The old Martham windmill

16
The Swithland Story

Alan Rowden

During the summer of 1987–8, a number of truly huge and fabulous rudd caught by the Culley family and Alan Rowden shocked the specimen-hunting world. When they found their way into the pages of the angling press, we were suddenly all poised waiting for the record to be toppled. Reported as coming from a Midlands' reservoir, the true venue for these catches was kept a secret to avoid upsetting the delicate nature of the fishing permit arrangements. As a consequence very few anglers ever learned the true story behind these incredible captures.

Alan Rowden is a regular contributor to the angling press and a tremendously successful all-round, big-fish specialist from Nottingham. For the first time ever, he tells the full story behind the huge and beautiful rudd from Swithland Reservoir.

Swithland Reservoir

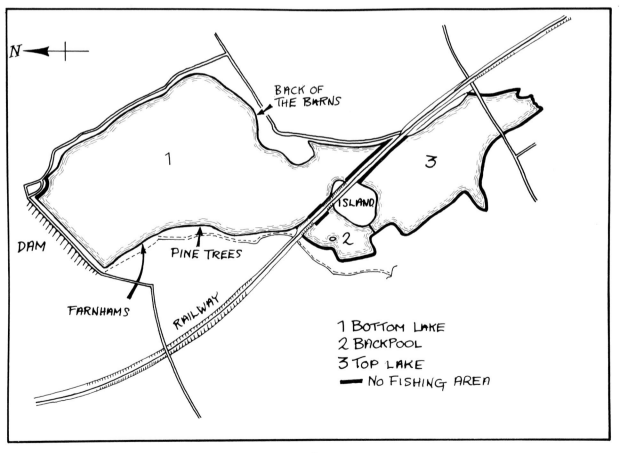

1 BOTTOM LAKE
2 BACKPOOL
3 TOP LAKE
— NO FISHING AREA

In the early seventies I joined up with a rather formidable band of anglers known as the Soar Valley Specimen Group with a view to generally broadening my angling interests, and hopefully increasing my repertoire of waters.

Bryan Culley, Andy Lister and other group members were, at the time, catching a quantity of big roach and pike from a water near to the group's headquarters at Quorn, in Leicestershire: the water was Swithland Reservoir. Unfortunately it became quickly apparent that access to the water was extremely difficult as only a handful of permits were available from the Earl of Lanesborough who owned the estate in which the water was situated. My only chance of fishing the water was as a guest of Bryan Culley but as my interests lay in fishing for chub in the winter, and carp and tench in the summer, the opportunity to fish the water did not present itself for at least two seasons.

Although Swithland is a very large water, it is dissected by the Great Central Railway which effectively creates three separate lakes. The lakes became known as the Main or Bottom Lake, the Top Lake, and the Backpool. Although the Main Lake and the Backpool are really one lake, they are actually separated by railway arches. The Top Lake is, however, properly enclosed from the Main Lake and the Backpool by means of a concrete silt trap although, at times of very high water, the silt trap is totally submerged and the three lakes merge.

I first fished the water in the mid-seventies when I joined Bryan Culley and John Noon for a pike-fishing session. Although it was a pleasant January day, I fully remember not being terribly impressed with the water. It seemed a wild and hostile place, and I found the water actually quite awesome as I was used to fishing more intimate, tranquil waters at the time. Over the next few years it was the excellent pike fishing which was at the forefront of the angling attention on the water, but every now and again the roach would show and a few big fish were taken by those who bothered to fish for them.

In the late seventies and early eighties a number of catches were made which, in isolation, were of little or no significance but collectively indicated that a new era was emerging on Swithland. In August 1978 a vast quantity of small fish were observed topping around the railway arches between the Main and Top Lakes. Out of curiosity Bryan and Andy decided to fish for them. Literally dozens of fish were caught on the float-fished maggots – like peas in a pod, they were all rudd around 6oz.

Then in July 1980, Andy was in need of some eel baits and decided to fish a swim on the Railway Bank which appeared to be teeming with small fish at the time. However, it wasn't a small fish which took Andy's float-fished maggot, it was a rudd of 2lb 3oz. This was followed by another 2-pounder; in all, Andy caught nine rudd that day from 1lb 6oz to 2lb 3oz. After this catch the rudd were not seen or even thought of for a number of years.

With the exception of the winter pike fishing, the water slid into a rather quiet period for a number of years until one evening in July 1983. Bryan and his two young sons, Jon and Steven, had returned to the reservoir after an abortive session elsewhere. They chose to fish an area on the south bank of the Main Lake known as the 'Back of the Barn'. Bryan remembers that there were large fish rolling everywhere, the water appeared to be alive with fish that night. Some of the fish were undoubtedly tench but Bryan thought that most of the fish were big roach. Later that night, Bryan had a bite on float-fished maggot. The fish was a very large rudd and weighed 2lb 12oz. It was

I had started my fishing on the Railway Bank

then that Bryan realised that most of the fish he had seen rolling the previous evening were actually rudd and not roach at all. Following this capture, both Bryan and Andy began to fish seriously for the rudd, although neither of them knew that they were witnessing the dawning of such a great era in angling history.

Over the next two seasons the rudd fed freely. Both Bryan and Andy amassed an impressive tally of big fish but it wasn't until the autumn of 1984 that Bryan's initial fish of 2lb 12oz was beaten, when Andy took a cracking fish of 2lb 15oz from the same area. Although the rudd came to the net at a steady pace, the fishing could never be described as being easy. The rudd themselves were not actually hard to catch but the general problems surrounding the fishing were always in evidence.

The areas allocated for fishing were only perhaps one half of the total bank space, so this obviously limited the choice of swims. Although, at the time, it was not really necessary to fish elsewhere, it would have been an asset to have had the choice. The other major problem concerned the night fishing. All the rudd had been caught during the hours of darkness, which was not actually allowed; however, Bryan and Andy had something of a gentleman's agreement with the keeper. This agreement was a rather delicate affair, especially where the guests were concerned. Fortunately prior to the start of the 1985/86 season, the Earl of Lanesborough lost his stranglehold on the fishing rights and I was able to obtain a permit and fish the water properly for the first time.

Left: 3lb 2oz of pure Swithland gold for Alan Rowden

Right: A massive brace of rudd weighing 3lb 10oz and 3lb 4oz

From the start of that next season a little more bank space was opened up for fishing. Bryan decided to concentrate on one of these new stretches which was called Farnhams and was soon into some big rudd, taking fish to 2lb 14oz in the first few weeks. I had started my fishing from a swim on the Railway Bank and, like Bryan, had also found some good fish with the best also going a very pleasing 2lb 14oz.

As the season progressed the rudd fishing became decidedly tedious but Bryan eventually broke new ground by taking the first fish over 3lb from the water, first with a fish of exactly 3lb, and then with a fish of 3lb 1oz. Following the capture of these fish the activity disappeared and eventually Bryan threw in the towel and went off to fish another water. I decided to persevere and in Bryan's absence I decided to fish on Farnhams for want of a change of scenery. On my second session in the new area I took my first 'three' from the water and a new lake record of 3lb 2oz. That fish turned out to be the last rudd to be taken from the water that season, as the night fishing was terminated shortly afterwards due to a rather unfortunate confrontation between two anglers and the keeper.

The following season started with a bang as Andy took a colossal fish of 3lb 8oz from Farnhams on opening night. It was only the previous season that we were contemplating the chance of a 3-pounder from the water – now we were thinking in terms of a possible 'four'. The rest of that summer we were handicapped by problem after problem. The night fishing had not been restored to its former level which severely limited our choice of swims but the greatest problem that year was almost continual algal bloom. The water would turn into a thick pea soup and fishing would become quite impossible. Despite all the problems we did manage to pick up the odd fish. I had been concentrating on a new area on the west bank of the Main Lake known as the 'Pine Trees'. I took several fish over 3lb up to 3lb 4oz, and Andy also took a big fish of 3lb 6oz. After the capture of these fish it was quite apparent that the average size of the rudd had increased noticeably since the previous season. We constantly asked ourselves, where would it end?

Rather true to form, the fishing at the Pine Trees lapsed into a series of quite monotonous blanks so Andy decided to try the Railway Bank for a change and soon located some rudd. After taking several 2-pounders Andy was joined by Bryan who had really struggled for much of the summer. On the last Sunday evening of September that season, Andy, Bryan and his son, Jon, settled into some swims on the Railway Bank for a short session. It was a warm, still end to the day as the threesome watched the light slowly ebb away. Shortly after 9pm Bryan had a bite on his bread and maggot cocktail. Initially Bryan thought he had hooked a tench, but after a short fight he landed a massive rudd. The fish weighed a staggering 4lb 2oz. That fish absolutely shattered us all, for many days afterwards we just could not believe it. Earlier in the season we were thinking of a possible 'four', now we were surely staring into the face of a record fish.

Before the start of the 1987/88 season, the night fishing had been almost fully restored. This meant that several of the previous hotspots could now be fished properly. The season started well, with Bryan, Andy, Jon and myself all taking some big tench in the opening few days but unfortunately the action was not to last. As the season progressed much of the time was spent generally scratching about in the hope that something would turn up somewhere. Bryan eventually caught the first rudd of the season which was a fish of 3lb 8oz from the Railway Bank. This fish appeared to be something of a loner for, despite a considerable degree of attention on the area of capture, no other fish were forthcoming and the water once again lapsed into a period of inactivity.

By the middle of July the lack of activity had persuaded Bryan and Andy to forsake the reservoir in favour of the delights of Trent carp fishing. At the beginning of the third week in July I lost a very big rudd in a swim on the Railway Bank. Desperate for revenge I returned the following evening and took two fish of 2lb 15oz and 3lb respectively. Those two rudd were the start of an incredible run of fish which I took from a number of different areas and culminated in a new personal best of 3lb 10oz from the Railway Bank. After this bonanza, Bryan and Andy were easily tempted away from the Trent, with the prospects of success on the reservoir now a distinct possibility.

Unfortunately things went rather quiet for a couple of weeks until Bryan and I fished the Pine Trees one Friday night. It promised to be a wild and windy night as we met at the water. Neither of us was too keen to fish due to the inclement weather, and a suggestion to retire to a nearby hostelry was seriously considered. Once we started to prepare our swims our spirits began to rise. We baited with crumb and maggots at a distance of about 40yd, in about 10ft of water. I fished straight flake in conjunction with an open-end feeder filled with bread and maggots. Bryan, on the other hand, fished his favourite bread and maggot cocktail and a block-end feeder.

I cast my first rod out over the baited area, and whilst I was baiting the second rod I

Surface-feeding rudd

had a stonking bite which was missed. It now became apparent that this was going to be one of those sessions. Shortly before midnight Bryan had a bite and also missed it but soon made amends when a little later he had another bite and duly landed a rudd of 2lb 11oz. After midnight things went rather quiet until around 1.30am. I had a slow bite and connected. Initially I was convinced that I had hooked a tench but as I drew the fish to the waiting net a large gold shape appeared on the surface. In a last attempt to escape the fish kited to the right and promptly shed the hook. Bitterly disappointed I persevered for an hour or so and then it started to rain – that really was the last straw! Bryan had also had enough so we decided to pack up and in the torrential rain we trudged back to our cars.

The following evening Bryan was working but I was eager to fish the Pine Trees again. I arrived at the water in good time to prepare the swim and get settled well before dark. The weather was much more agreeable than it had been the previous evening, although it was still fairly breezy. I decided to fish the swim which Bryan had fished the previous night as it was a little more sheltered. Finally settled I watched the light gradually slip away and, with great anticipation, I waited for the 'hot' period of 10pm to midnight: 10pm came and went as I hovered over my rods in an atmosphere which can only be described as electric. I sat listening to the constant cacophany of 50,000 gulls roosting in the centre of the lake when around 11.30pm I began to get single bleeps on my optonics. These were accompanied by short lifts on the bobbins and were a sure sign that fish were in the swim. Gradually the activity increased until suddenly one of the optonics erupted and the bobbin smashed to the rod and I was 'in'. The rod arched over as 40yd out in the blackness, I felt the satisfying 'thump', 'thump' of a big rudd.

I played the fish carefully until it was safely in the net. My initial estimate of the fish was that it was around 4lb but my scales said 3lb 10oz. I couldn't understand why such a huge fish could weigh so little. Over the next half an hour I missed two or three finicky sorts of bite, then I had a very deliberate drop back and connected with another big rudd. This fish was marginally smaller and weighed a respectable 3lb 4oz. After that fish I cast out in the hope of more action but the fish had gone.

As daylight broke I was joined by Keith Salter who had now started to fish with us (Keith had not seen a big rudd before). As he did the honours with the cameras he appeared to be quite stunned. It was Keith who caught several high 'twos' over the next few weeks as he christened his career in Swithland rudd fishing. The night fishing ended at the end of August and on the last weekend I capped a memorable summer with another cracking brace of rudd going to 3lb 8oz and 3lb 5oz from the Railway Bank.

At the beginning of the 1988/89 season we all started tench fishing. This was of a very high standard while it lasted but rather predictably the tench did their disappearing act at the beginning of July. To try and locate some fish we all started trying different areas. This move seemed to be largely unsuccessful until one evening Bryan and Jon found some fish rolling in a large bay on the east bank of the Main Lake. There seemed to be both tench and rudd rolling in some numbers so the duo found suitable swims and set up, confident that they were going to catch. Although the rolling continued well after dark, not a bobbin stirred.

Some time after midnight Jon's optonic burst into life and, as quite often happens, Jon thought he had hooked a tench. As the fish rolled in the margins it became obvious that the fish was a rudd, and a very big rudd indeed. The fish weighed 4lb 5oz and was the second biggest rudd caught in this country. The following evening Bryan returned to fish the swim alone and again the area was alive with fish. Bryan fished his usual bread and maggot cocktail in conjunction with a block-end feeder of maggots, on both rods. After darkness had fallen, Bryan caught a monster which weighed exactly 4lb. Bryan sacked the fish and as there were still fish rolling he hurriedly cast out in the hope of further action. Unfortunately after a while the swim appeared to die and Bryan's confidence began to wane. As the early morning sky began to lighten Bryan had another bite: this fish was also a very big rudd weighing an impressive 3lb 14oz. With this fantastic brace of fish Bryan was overwhelmed. Following the news of these two sensational catches we all began to concentrate on the area as it was obvious that a very heavy concentration of fish were in the bay. Although several smaller rudd fell to Bryan and Jon over the next few days, the fishing rather characteristically declined into a series of eventless blanks.

Several weeks passed by without a hint of the rudd either rolling or feeding, the water had now entered the quietest period that we could remember. Gradually, one by one, the gang surrendered to the uphill struggle, like slain warriors on the battlefield – Bryan, Jon and Andy drifted off to pastures new. It was Keith and myself who persevered as the addiction to the water grew stronger.

Weeks grew into months without a bite, or even the slightest hint of a fish moving. As with previous seasons the feeling of 'tomorrow night could be the one' was the only solace in the endless series of blanks. Eventually it was a swim on the Railway Bank that rescued me from the brink of insanity when one evening Keith and I spotted some rolling rudd. It seemed so easy as I took fish of 3lb 8oz, 3lb 6oz and 3lb in two evening sessions, but predictably the action was very brief, for shortly after the initial location the rudd disappeared like ghosts in the night. Poor old Keith fishing alongside me failed to catch. At the end of August the night fishing ended and effectively terminated the rudd fishing for another year. Keith had probably fished harder than any of us, and though a very competent angler, he failed to catch a single rudd. This is a measure of how heartbreaking the water can be.

Swithland is no ordinary water. It is, without doubt, a water which holds some legendary fish, but rarely gives up its secrets. On a warm summer evening it is a water of immense beauty and unparalleled tranquility; it is a water for the dreamer; it is a water for Ratty and Mole; a water for Bilbo and Frodo. When I first saw the water I was unimpressed – I was so very wrong for even after a short time the water began to grow on me and, as with my companions, it rapidly became an obsession.

The Swithland story has not only been about success, it has been about good friends and companionship, and about people pulling together. There has been competition and the occasional envy, but there have also been practical jokes and much laughter. All in all I feel rather privileged to have been there.

Chris Turnbull 89

17

Llandegfedd: The Instant Legend

Robert Jones

Living in South Wales, Bob Jones is one of angling's less prominent public figures. Despite this he has been tremendously successful over the years. Twice, in fact, he has caught record-breaking eels which weighed 8lb ½oz and 7lb 8oz respectively. As one of the Redmire syndicate in the seventies, he took carp to 38lb 12oz, a fish which eventually grew to become Yates's record.

Along with his close friend Pete Climo, we have Bob to thank for his tireless campaigning to open Llandegfedd Reservoir for pike fishing. A campaign which led to the birth of an instant legend and a Mecca for the pike-angling world. It was an event which lasted for two weeks only, and which unfortunately was cancelled the following year due to drought conditions, but despite this the pike record was almost toppled not just once but on four occasions.

Llandegfedd Reservoir is one of those places which paints a picture on one's mind of a gentle giant whose surface shimmers like a million diamonds in the gentle breezes of spring and summer. The waters always seem blue and benign, never raging and storm tossed, like some malevolent monster, eagerly seeking a life to extinguish as so many large bodies of water do. On approaching it, from high above at the southern end, it overwhelms the senses in an instant. Nestling snugly in the rolling, wooded hills of central Gwent it appears suddenly, like an oasis in a desert. Tucked away in the valley of the Sor Brook this beautiful and magic place seems so far removed from the industrial areas of South Wales which are only a footstep away. Indeed, an oasis it is for it is the largest body of stillwater, containing coarse fish, in Gwent and most of Wales.

It is well established now with its 435 acres edged by a variety of beautiful, wild wooded and scrubby areas and by farmed field and pasture. Once it was completed and filled in 1966 it looked, even then, as though it had always been there. Exactly as it looks today, there were no raw edges or eyesores to be covered, all was 'perfect'. Yet this whole picture is merely an illusion for the stream, which was dammed to provide such a beautiful lake, is totally inadequate to maintain water levels against the demands by the consumer and there is constant need for compensation. This is provided by regular pumped supplies from the River Usk some miles to the east.

The basin for the reservoir was constructed in a bed of limestone and slate which provide alkaline conditions so beneficial to all aquatic species. Its depths plunge to over 120ft at the southern end, near the dam, though the northern half only reaches around 65ft. Despite the depths and steeply sloping bottom it has, over the years, supported an abundance of fish life. The best example of this is demonstrated by the fact that sacks full of dace have been removed from the draw-off filter screens at 20, 60, 90 and 120ft! Whoever would contemplate dace fishing at that depth? He'd need a long pole!

Soon after the reservoir opened it was providing exciting sport with small brown

An abundance of massive pike

trout around 1lb apiece. These fish, however, were shortly to succumb to the ravages of the salmon disease UDN (ulcerative dermal necrosis) which entered the water via the pumping system. It was then stocked with rainbows to maintain the Welsh custom and practice of game fisheries only. The stocking densities have tended to be mediocre and the trout fishing followed suit, with little signs of large fish appearing. Until, that is, one of the regular trout anglers began to return with large brownies of 6, 7, 8 and 9lb in weight. Fisheries staff became suspicious and watched closely as he fished in the secluded Sor Bay: they discovered that this most amazing man was taking them on worm-baited hand-lines. This illegal act was the first real indication of the water's ability to produce large carniverous specimens and it's certain that many larger brownies exist there to this day.

Contemplating Llandegfedd from the car park high above the dam at the south-eastern corner, it is always easy to imagine vast numbers of all sorts of species and envisage leviathans of all kinds moving gently along the bottom in search of some tasty morsel. In fact, there is a large selection of species present which, in the main, reflect those found in the Usk system so it isn't difficult to work out how they arrived there. How bream, tench and rudd appeared is a little more difficult to explain, however, but it's fairly easy to guess. Species present are trout (brown and rainbow), roach, dace, chub, perch, gudgeon, bullhead, eels, lampreys, pike, bream, tench and rudd. Roach and dace appeared in large numbers very shortly after the opening and the pike soon after that. Other species have become more prolific in the ensuing years. The dominant species are now roach, dace, perch and pike.

Kevin Clifford wet and beaming – with a 36lb Llandegfedd monster

Apart from those large, illegally caught brown trout early hints of 'specimens' came from fisheries staff, who used to net brownies, at spawning time, for breeding purposes. They claimed to have taken numbers of fish in excess of 10lb to an estimated 15lb, a good fish by any standards. Though most fish reach a relatively low average size, the roach appear to be most suited to the reservoir for shoals are vast and the average size is large. During the drought summer of 1976 the water level plummeted, like so many others, to an all-time low and revealed, in no uncertain terms, the roach fishing potential of this lake. Sor Bay, with its trickle of oxygenated water, was a sight to behold for the roach pushed and jostled to cram themselves, as tightly as possible, into the area of highest oxygen content. They were there in thousands, I really believe it would have been possible to walk over their backs. What astonished me though was the size because most appeared to be well in excess of 1lb. They weren't any old roach, tattered and worn from excessive capture and age, they were immaculate, deep bodied, glowing silver and blue with perfect red fins and scales like sixpenny pieces (remember those?). I never saw one under 1lb but I saw many over 2lb.

Llandegfedd Reservoir

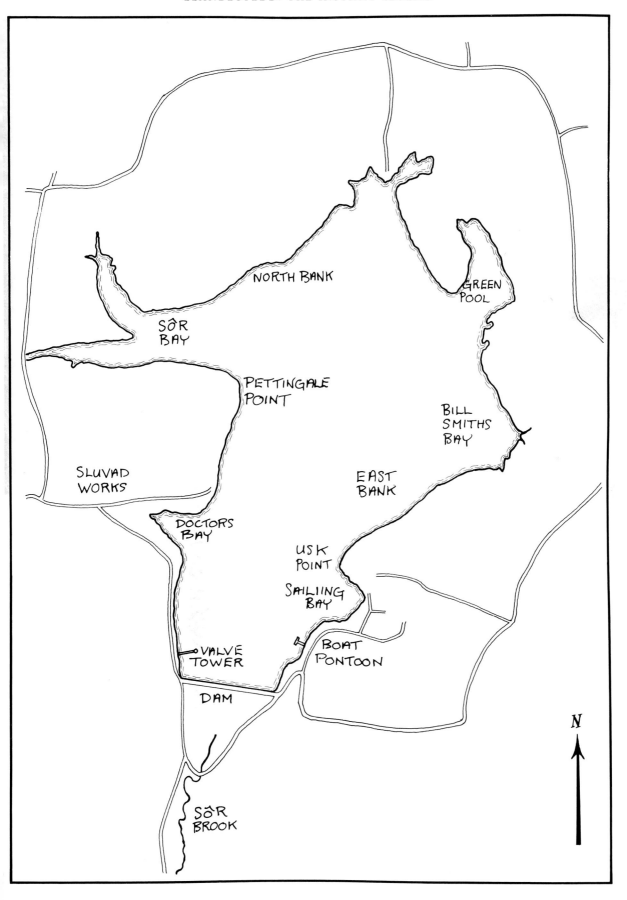

For many years the reservoir has been the preserve of trout anglers who have been permitted to fish fly only. Other activities have been allowed for various bodies with interests in water sports and such like. The exception to this was, inevitably, coarse angling. Such an important body of water was quickly adopted by the local naturalists and ornithologists for it soon proved to be a fairly important site for wintering wildfowl. The result was that the Nature Conservancy Council was quickly involved and it was declared a Site of Special Scientific Interest, closing it to virtually all surface and bank activity during the winter months. Angling was permitted, generally, from mid-March or early April until the middle of October. Prior to 1988 the only break from tradition was when a series of coarse angling trials was held in October and November of 1977.

That series of trials was held, by dictate from the Welsh Water Authority, in areas considered unsuitable for successful coarse angling by the average matchmen, and so it was. What was very important, though, was that the authority had conceded and given way to pressure and sound argument from the coarse sector. This was a monumental break from tradition which set an important precedent in a system which hitherto would not have even considered bending to the wishes of such an 'important' group. Such an event, though ending in failure, strengthened the resolve of those who knew the reservoir's potential and provided us with the inspiration to maintain pressure until the water could be opened for all to share. Despite the now well-documented events of 1988 the battle continues. Pressure was maintained by the local coarse-angling fraternity in an effort to gain a share in a facility which was, after all, an undersubscribed public amenity. As the years passed many lost interest as their confidence waned but one or two were prepared to continue with unwavering enthusiasm because they realised the true potential of the place and felt determined to put right a great injustice. There was good reason for the frustration and feelings of failure because it really did appear that the trout anglers, not the authority's officers, were the decision-makers. Two events occurred in 1986 and 1987 which set the wheels of progress in motion very rapidly indeed.

Over the years there had been a protracted policy of culling all coarse fish species to maintain a 'balanced' (?) fishery for the game anglers. During this time larger and larger pike were being taken and destroyed until, in 1985, five pike over 30lb were taken out. The crunch came, however, in 1986 when, during the spring, five fish in excess of 40lb were removed, with the largest reported at 45lb 12oz. In addition to those magnificent creatures there were more reported to be in excess of 30lb. Such an abundance of massive pike, plus those of previous years, was unheard of in the history of British pike habitats. Though not an ideal solution by any means, the fish trapped in 1986 were not killed but removed to other waters in the hope that they would thrive and provide sport for pike anglers. They never did!

The reason for the change of policy was a telephone conversation between Dr Graeme Harris and myself following the destruction of those huge fish in 1985. Dr Harris, the principal fisheries officer, agreed that such an act was a waste of valuable resources and directed his staff to try and find suitable alternative homes for future captives. However, following the 1986 results I spoke to him again on the same issue: pike trapping and wasted potential. We discussed the fantastic opportunity being lost and the obvious detrimental effects such dramatic reductions of large predators must inevitably have on the water. Again Dr Harris acted decisively, if belatedly, by implementing a policy of trapping, tagging and release for future years to build up an

Stuart Gilham with Britain's third biggest pike, weighing a fantastic 44lb

accurate picture of population and growth rates. In retrospect, it is clear that the writing was on the wall.

Water levels and weather conditions seemed to be responsible for shortage of spawning fish during 1987. Green Pool and along North Shore, where fyke nets were usually laid were, much of the time, left high and dry as the water dropped rapidly thus few fish were taken. The spectacular catches of the previous two seasons weren't repeated but fish to 36lb were taken nevertheless. It's hardly surprising really when one considers that such large numbers of very large fish were removed previously and that's not counting others in double figures including some over 20lb. 1988 was similar in a number of respects but fish to a reported 48lb were taken and tagged. Shortly after the trout season opened one of the anglers found a huge pike dead in the margins of Sor Bay. Realising this was something rather special he measured it to relay the information to a local pike angler. It was 53in from tip of snout to fork of tail; its weight, anybody's guess.

Let's return to 1987 for a moment, for I believe this to be a very significant time in the history of Llandegfedd. During the early part of that year the management of the reservoir was taken over by John Davies who was based at WWA offices in Mid-Glamorgan. He had been in charge of fisheries work at Pontsticill Reservoir some years previously and put into practice the monumental and progressive idea of shared trout and coarse angling. It proved successful with no conflict! He also introduced a rule stipulating that all pike over 7lb were to be returned to the water. Clearly this was in the interests of sound management principles but, more importantly, it was previously unheard of in Wales. John has a well-developed sense of fair play and a willingness to consider both sides of an argument on their merits. I have the highest respect and a great regard for this man.

I have not the slightest doubt that John's involvement with Llandegfedd led to the rapid series of positive moves which culminated in the decision to open the reservoir for pike-fishing trials during 1988. The final decision, taken in September 1987, was confirmed in April 1988 and arrangements were made to open the water, to pike anglers, for the last two weeks of October in the same year. Owing to my regular contacts with the angling press, John asked me to inform *Angling Times.* The news which the specimen world had awaited so long was received with a buzz of excitement. The telephone lines to the Llandegfedd ranger's office were jammed solid within hours.

Regulations regarding the forthcoming trial were, to say the least, a little restrictive but the methods were known pike 'killers'. To begin with only twenty of the forty boats were available for booking but any remaining after 11 October were to be eligible for trout or pike bookings. There was to be no bank fishing and all anglers had to be in possession of a current trout rod-licence and purchase a trout-fishing permit. Fishing was to be limited to one rod with lures or sea-fish dead-baits being the acceptable methods. All this, incredibly, was designed to placate those trout anglers who continued to believe that this was all a ploy to steal their trout. It's hard to credit that so many believed such absolute nonsense!

Tuesday, 18 October 1988 was the opening day of what were to prove fourteen days of pure magic. The first day alone would have made Llandegfedd a legend; it certainly began the writing of one of the most important chapters in Britain's pike-angling history. Most of the boats were booked by pike anglers and the day dawned with clear, frosty skies and a blanket of fog over land and water. The surface was calm and largely invisible. It was, in a word, the pike angler's nightmare . . . Yet it was to prove a dream! Assembled on the banks ready to launch the new 'Armada' were men who were unknown, experienced and inexperienced, and men who were not only known but had already become legends in their own lifetimes. Yet, even now, after years of publicity, there were many who still did not believe but who later realised the folly of such disbelief. No one could have known what the day had in store but there were secret thoughts of 'thirties,' 'forties', personal bests and even that elusive record – and so it was to be. *Angling Times* had the wisdom and foresight to send a team of reporters and pike experts: Eddie Turner, Vic Gibson and Stuart Gilham. Foolishly, the other papers did not!

Reminiscent of the D-Day landings the mass of boats roared and jerked off into the mist as the engines and oars exerted their mastery over the cool, clear waters. Some, with prior knowledge, headed for areas they knew or suspected would hold fish, others used their echo sounders whilst a few just stopped on spec. Perhaps it was more than pure coincidence that the majority stopped in around 35ft of water some 200yd off the north shore. What happened next is history now but during that first day fish of 12lb, 14lb, 22lb, 23lb, 32lb, 33lb 6oz, 33lb 12oz and 44lb 8oz came to the net. The record hadn't been beaten but it had been shaken rigid. Telephone lines around the country became red hot, Llandegfedd was to be on the angling world's lips for weeks to come.

John Culley was the first person known to have taken a fish, his largest to date; it was caught on a lure and scaled 33lb 6oz. Like all of the others it was pristine, deep and solid bodied with golden flanks and perfect fins. These fish had, largely, never felt hooks before and had certainly not encountered such devastating methods and tackle. All fought deep, long and hard determined to gain their cherished freedom but all finally gave in to a superior adversary. Llandegfedd had passed the test by early afternoon because, by then, Carl Garratt had landed a huge fish of 44lb 8oz on float-fished herring which, I am told, was dyed with coloured stripes. Pike history had been rewritten after only one day. Wales, the country so long written-off by the specimen-hunting fraternity, struck back with a vengeance during the next thirteen days showing that it possessed not only an exceptional pike-fishery but, a new Mecca, the best in the land.

Each day saw the same performance as the anglers hurled their boats across the lake in a fever of excitement, barely contained and openly exhibited. Some faces changed but many stayed for virtually the whole of the time. They were generally well behaved and abided by the rigid leaving and return times. The water authority rangers were tolerant, unobtrusive and delighted with everything that happened. Even so, four anglers were banned, two permanently, for malpractice. Nevertheless those who fished

gained a huge vote of respect from all of the water authority officers and did much to show many of the trout anglers that co-existence is possible. Many have said how impressed they were by the obvious care and concern shown when handling captured pike and by the attention to detail when preparing tackle and equipment. Eyes have been opened, new links have been forged even though some are reluctant to admit it in public.

Throughout the period of fishing, South Wales was suffering its coldest spell of the 1988/89 winter with clear skies, heavy frosts and morning mists (I write this in January/February 1989). However, despite many people's lack of confidence in such conditions, day two produced one fish of 34lb and three others over 20lb, the largest going 28lb 12oz. Sadly that fish was killed the following day because it was still floating belly up and a 34lb fish died a week or so after the trial ended. Third time lucky was the watchword for day three when five 'thirties', nine 'twenties' and some doubles were taken. It was on this day that the effectiveness of those weird and wonderful Pierce and Bumble-Bee lures was to show itself head and shoulders above so many others. Using these the *Angling Times* team produced a splendid trio of fish scaling 34½lb (Mark Williams), 36lb (Mick Rouse) and 36½lb (Dave Chilman), the two biggest being played from the same boat at the same time. The latter proved a short-lived, lure-caught record. Depending on your point of view, Max Cottis had the best bag that day, four fish over 20lb. The halcyon days, both weather and fish wise, lasted until the Saturday (day five) but in between times Steve Gould of T.G. Lures made his mark with five fish over 20lb on the same day. Saturday, like the others, provided its share of humour and amazement – local angler Will Travers came out of five years' retirement and produced a personal best of 31lb within about an hour. Andy Mundy asked Lyn Bulley for a go on the lure on which he'd just taken specimens of 24lb and 27lb. He cast out and promptly hooked a fish of 30lb 8oz. The crunch came when Stuart Gilham's slowly retrieved sardine was grabbed by a heavyweight which, after an arm-aching ten minutes or so, rolled into the net to be greeted by a loud shout of joy from Stuart. The huge fish was taken ashore and weighed carefully at 44lb exactly. Subsequently investigation showed it to be a different fish from Carl Garratt's.

From now on the fish proved elusive, they had taken one hell of a hammering and didn't want to play ball any more. Llandegfedd grudgingly continued to give up some 'superfish'. Andy Trimm took one of 28lb 4oz on the eighth day and his boat partner Brian Ingram latched into a beauty of 43lb 2oz on the following day. That one was eventually identified as Stuart's fish. A 29lb 12oz came out, to local man Phil Pearson, next day on a bait laying-on in 10ft of water. The final day dawned much the same as the others but there was little activity except for a good fish being lost, until the end of the afternoon. A more just and fitting end couldn't have been imagined when my regular pike-angling companion, Pete Climo, hit a big one during the last hour. After something of a dour struggle he landed Carl Garratt's fish, from day one, but now it scaled 42lb 5oz. It had lost some weight but still merits the distinction of the most reliably authenticated, largest lure-caught British pike. There's no doubt who is prettier in the photographs either.

Spirits were high and everything was good natured throughout the fortnight. Old friendships were renewed and many new ones created. The fishing sounds easy and so it was for some but many fished without a twitch, so for others it was very hard. It was largely a question of being in the right place at the right time, often numbers of fish came to only a few well-placed boats. Results were outstanding, a 'new' fishery had been pioneered by those men and they'd rewritten the books. Many have asked where the small fish were, why such an imbalance? Small ones were caught, though – perhaps the honours on this one should go to Chris Tarrant with one of 1lb 12oz.

Final totals at Llandegfedd, for the first trial, will never be known absolutely accurately but my records show something in the order of fifty fish over 20lb with fifteen of them above 30lb and four of those over 40lb. Only two tagged pike were taken, so where were the other twenty or so? Why has Llandegfedd proved to be such an outstanding fishery? What weight was the huge fish, nicknamed the 'Dolphin', which cavorted on the surface, like so many of the big fish, when things were quiet? Such questions may never be answered but some guesses can be made. Despite the long-running discussions and opinions about the reasons for trout-fishery pike being so large, I still believe that feeding on the trout is a secondary factor. To my way of thinking, Jim Gibbinson hit the nail on the head some years ago when he conjectured that pike, and pike fisheries, thrive on neglect. Llandegfedd is twenty-two years old, netting has always been fraught with difficulties and they have never been fished for with rod and line. There are vast shoals of coarse fish in the lime-rich water and authority research has shown these to be the staple food of the pike. Finally, the fluctuating water levels, in spring, have probably often resulted in destruction of the spawn which has served to regulate the biomass of pike to a lower number of individuals.

The 'Dolphin', which cavorted on the surface

Regardless of the hypotheses it is obvious that these fish must now be protected and carefully managed (neglected even) to maintain the superlative standards of fishing. The Welsh Water Authority has recognised that this is a 'discovery' of major importance, now considered the jewel in the crown. That jewel must be locked away and brought out at rare intervals to be polished, admired and nurtured. But wait, that's a selfish view because it doesn't really matter any more – or does it? Llandegfedd Reservoir is now written into the folklore of British angling – from day one it had become a legend!

Postscript

On 9 and 10 March 1990 a small number of anglers took part in a scientific assessment experiment, run by Welsh Water, to try to find the true potential of the pike in Llandegfedd. Rather than use nets, which could damage the fish, it was decided to use rod and line. In short, this would be an attempt to bring the record to Llandegfedd.

Invitations were restricted in the main to selected Welsh Water staff and directors, but three pike angling experts were also asked to participate; Fred Buller, Bob Jones and Pete Climo.

At 9am on the first day, Welsh international rugby star Gareth Edwards (fishing under the guidance of Bob Jones) caught his first ever 20lb-plus pike on a large silver Mepps spinner from the entrance to Green Pool. It weighed 45lb 6oz and set a new record for the species. The fish was not recognised as being one of the forties taken in the 1988 pike fishing trial, and one can only guess at how much one of those would weigh with a full roe at the back end of the season.

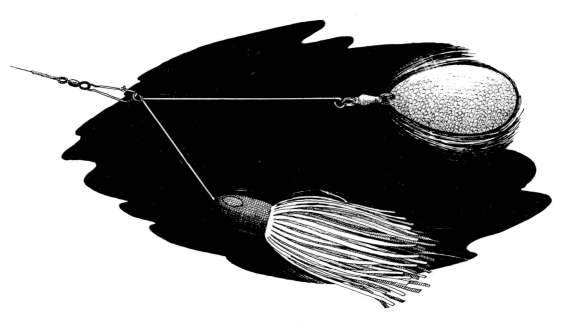

Conclusion: Into the Nineties

Chris Turnbull

And so as another decade comes to an end the question arises 'What of the future?' Nothing, of course, remains constant in angling. New opportunities arise and old haunts fade into fond memories. Some patterns, however, do exist and therefore it is possible to make a few guesses at what the nineties may bring.

Our rivers are certainly under real pressure, and we may be the generation to witness the outcome of their appalling decline, which has been evident throughout the eighties in so many places. The fabulous roach of the Wensum, for instance, could possibly now be a thing of the past. The Hampshire Avon, too, may well be irreversibly on its way out. While its big fish peak at the moment it is difficult to put things in perspective. With sewage consents and abstraction licences reaching an all time high, it is difficult to be optimistic. However, the EEC will demand that some real action is taken, and the British government and the water authorities surely cannot resist forever. The 'Green' movement is also now getting stuck into the water issues. In the mid-eighties that was an area which was really only the concern of anglers, but by 1989 it had become an issue of massive public concern – 'a real hot potato' – and of national importance, so maybe there is now some light at the end of the tunnel. Anglers *must* shrug off their terrible complacency, for there is so much they can do if they want to secure a brighter future for these legendary rivers.

On the Wensum, the Norfolk Anglers Conservation Association is constantly challenging the water environment issues. Pollution, though temporarily devastating, can be stopped; but it is only one of our worries. Habitat destruction in the long run may be a far larger problem for our fisheries. The association therefore has started a project of habitat improvements on its own section of the river. By constructing shallow gravel riffles on the river bed, an elevation of the flow is re-created, thus amending some of the inherent problems caused by dredging forty years ago. On these riffles food supplies will build up and spawning facilities will improve. Bankside willows are being planted to create cover and trap floating reed rafts, thus providing suitable habitat for adult chub, barbel and roach. Selective weed cutting is now being taken on by the association rather than allowing the authorities to indiscriminately denude the river of all aquatic plant life, as they have done for many years.

Maybe schemes such as this can pave a way forwards. How much of this can be done throughout the country, of course, depends on the willingness of anglers to participate in the work and perhaps more importantly to fight to get things done. This would give our rivers a real boost, but even that is only tinkering and experimenting. Population dynamics of river fish need to be understood far more thoroughly than at present, and real hard cash must be spent if we are ever to really understand and solve the problems of declining stocks.

Now that the new National Rivers Authority has been formed, perhaps the complacency of the water authorities will be amended. Pollution must be tackled firmly, with the polluters being made to pay, and real co-operation with anglers must be achieved. There is some evidence of this happening now and although these are still early days, perhaps there is now at least a glimmer of hope for our fading rivers.

As long as we have good clean water, we will have our legendary fisheries. The pressures against them will be enormous and will force angling into becoming far more conservation-orientated. One organisation we will have to rely on more and more is the Anglers Co-operative Association, which is perhaps our only effective way of fighting pollution. If you haven't done so by now, do yourself a favour and join them.

On a more positive note, let's speculate a little on what we may have to look forward to during the nineties. Privatisation of the water authorities (while not a popular notion) could have some bright points and may in some ways give angling a few new opportunities. If profits are to be maximised, resources such as the reservoirs will need to be opened up far more to accommodate recreational interests. Angling as a whole surely will benefit from that, and as a result pike fishing on these vast waters may well become far more accessible; experiments such as the one on Llandegfedd could become regular events all around the country. Who knows, perhaps even the pike culling will be stopped eventually and the true pike potential of these waters be allowed to blossom. Maybe this is just a pipe dream, but how can anyone profit from having these potentially brilliant mixed fisheries unfished and wasted throughout the trout fishing close season? If they were to open their gates regularly to pikers, we might find that our long cherished 40-pounders are not quite as rare as supposed; and who knows, perhaps even those 'impossible' 50-pounders will become a reality.

The gravel extraction industry, for certain, will not be going out of business for the foreseeable future. Consequently more and more pits are constantly popping up all around the country. As far as angling is concerned, the benefits are obvious. With so many new pits, some are bound to be exceptional; the 15 and even 16lb bream of Queenford, for instance, may possibly become merely another stepping stone to ever bigger specimens from other waters, just as the TC fish were, once Alastair Nicholson had put Queenford on the map. Tench, too, will obviously benefit, as will all stillwater species, but it is the carp anglers who will ultimately reap the rewards. With the high priority carp stocking has received throughout the last twenty years we can surely expect new waters to emerge which could upstage Yateley and Savay. Just before this book was completed, Martin Gay took a 48lb common carp from an unexploited water. It was the nation's biggest ever by 4lb and was supported by the capture of numerous 20 and 30lb specimens. At present its location is still a secret; however, nothing stays a secret for ever in angling and once that water starts to receive attention it could well shine out as the ultimate big carp water. Doubtless other new waters will rise up like this and shock the carp angling world; perhaps one of them will produce a fish to topple Yates' 51.

One species, the wels catfish, never made its way into this book's pages. Claydon may be an exceptional water by English catfishing standards, but in reality it is merely a mediocre pond full of stunted kittens when compared with the potential for the species as seen in Europe. Catfish however have been moved around the country into many waters, and new stocks have been imported both legally and otherwise from abroad. Perhaps it is too early to see the ultimate results of these stockings come to fruition in the nineties, but it will surely bring about a new status for this exciting

The possibility of some very big cats being caught

species. One thing we cannot possibly deny, however, is the possibility of some very big cats being caught – at least by English standards. They could even become one of the most popular species by the end of the nineties.

Another alien species, the zander, is now surely in almost every river system in England. Love them or loathe them, they are here to stay. Through the nineties we may well see a real resurgence of zander fishing, not just on the Fens but on all the other waters in which they are becoming established. Twenty pounds is unlikely to be a barrier to their growth potential and we could well see some real monsters turning up. Thirty pounds is not impossible; after all, they grow bigger than that throughout most of Europe. It is easy to speculate, but in the final analysis only time will tell.

Should a zander boom such as this take place, I guess it could even be feasible that we may end up with an organisation dedicated purely to their capture. With the present-day ill-feeling that is piled against them, they will certainly need it!

Angling went through major changes in the eighties. Specialist organisations such as the National Association of Specialist Anglers, and the Carp Society, grew and blossomed to protect the interests of their members. The sport not only flourished, but found a new professionalism. Anglers were no longer seen to be the same bucolic characters they had been in the past (a harmless fool on one end of a string and a worm on the other). The sport fought its way through a wave of anti-angling public feelings (hostility which it probably deserved), but anglers won through to fight another day, and altogether angling's future should be all the stronger for it.

With the forward thinking of the Angling Foundation, the NASA and other associations which are taking the initiative to educate children into taking an aware attitude to their fishing, new generations will hopefully become ambassadors for the sport – the caring anglers of the future. A few youngsters already are creating names for themselves as successful big fish anglers, and no doubt the keenest will become the stars of the nineties. Others, perhaps even younger, may even now be innocently mocking their heroes – men like Rod Hutchinson, Neville Fickling and Richie McDonald – in just the same way my childhood friends and I once mocked Richard Walker and Fred Taylor, the stars of our own youth, whilst at the same time we tried to emulate their successes. We should wish them well, remembering it is our duty to help them not only to achieve their dreams but also to make sure they keep a clear perspective which will guide them through a lifetime of angling. One thing I desperately hope is that in this age of sleeping over bolt-rigs for carp and drowning deadbaits for pike they should remember that there is a whole world of possibilities out there to be experienced, both in our rivers and stillwaters. To lose sight of that is to remain only half awake to the diverse richness of this superb sport.

One thing is for sure: whatever their attitudes and whatever else happens, given half a chance a few of our waters will always rise far above the mediocre to attain great new heights. God willing, we will make them the legends of the nineties, legends every bit as fabulous as those through the eighties, and maybe, perhaps very occasionally, even a little greater still.